The Desire of Divine Love

Studies in Church History

William L. Fox
General Editor

Vol. 4

PETER LANG
New York • Washington, D.C./Baltimore • San Francisco
Bern • Frankfurt am Main • Berlin • Vienna • Paris

Leanne Van Dyk

The Desire of Divine Love

John McLeod Campbell's Doctrine of the Atonement

PETER LANG
New York • Washington, D.C./Baltimore • San Francisco
Bern • Frankfurt am Main • Berlin • Vienna • Paris

Library of Congress Cataloging-in-Publication Data

Van Dyk, Leanne.
 The desire of divine love: John McLeod Campbell's doctrine of the
atonement / Leanne Van Dyk.
  p.   cm. — (Studies in church history: vol. 4)
 Includes bibliographical references and index.
  1. Atonement. 2. Campbell, John McLeod, 1800–1872. Nature of the
atonement and its relation to remission of sins and eternal life. I. Title.
II. Series: Studies in church history (New York, N.Y.); vol. 4.
 BT265.2.V36   232′.3—dc20   94-30671
 ISBN 0-8204-2647-4
 ISSN 1074-6749

Die Deutsche Bibliothek-CIP-Einheitsaufnahme

Van Dyk, Leanne:
The desire of divine love: John McLeod Campbell's doctrine of the atonement
/ Leanne Van Dyk - New York; Washington, D.C./Baltimore; San Francisco;
Bern; Frankfurt am Main; Berlin; Vienna; Paris: Lang.
 (Studies in church history; Vol. 4)
 ISBN 0-8204-2647-4
NE: GT

Cover Design by James F. Brisson.

© 1995 Peter Lang Publishing, Inc., New York

Printed in the United States of America.

To Steven and Rachel

"The atonement is to be regarded
as that by which God has bridged over the gulf
which separated between what sin had made us,
and what it was the desire of the divine love
that we should become."

John McLeod Campbell

"For it ought not to be difficult to believe
that, though we have sinned against God,
God still regards us with a love
which has survived our sins."

John McLeod Campbell

CONTENTS

INTRODUCTION

The doctrine of the atonement has been the focus of renewed interest in recent years. Some interpretations of this premier Christian doctrine have constructed the atonement in innovative ways in an attempt to address the concerns of feminism, ecology and Christian-Jewish dialogue.[1] Liberation theologians continue to do theological reflection from their context of economically and politically oppressive systems and thus interpret the atonement in ways that give meaning particularly to the sufferings and death of Christ.[2] Still others are reexamining and reappropriating traditional models of atonement theology in an effort to maintain continuity with the tradition.[3]

This book will join the growing discussion on atonement by focusing on the atonement theology of John McLeod Campbell, nineteenth century Scottish Presbyterian pastor/theologian and author of *The Nature of the Atonement* (1856), a text which has exercised wide influence on subsequent Scottish and British atonement theologians.[4] There are several reasons why a critical analysis of Campbell's atonement theology is a valuable contribution to the current lively discussion on atonement doctrine.

First, one immediately is struck by the wide range of opinion on John McLeod Campbell's atonement theology. Orthodox, conservative, or evangelical Campbell interpreters tend to distance themselves from Campbell, thinking him to be dangerously "subjective."[5] Liberal or progressive interpreters feel kinship with Campbell on account of their perception of his subjective, experiential approach.[6] An assorted variety of other Campbell interpreters believe his work, in essence, is in strong continuity with the Reformed tradition and with Calvin, one who returned to the primary theological motivations of Calvin while avoiding the strongly penal emphases of the Federal Calvinists.[7] A new interpretive analysis of Campbell's atonement theology is called for in the light of such widely divergent appraisals.

In addition, careful interpretive analysis on Campbell's use of such terms as "perfect repentance" and his understanding of key atonement concepts like substitution and satisfaction is required. Furthermore, a study which attempts both to interpret his theory and place it in its broader theological context is necessary.

Critical to an accurate understanding of Campbell's atonement theology is a full appreciation for the role of specific foundational axioms or theological principles on his complete atonement theory. The role, especially, of the principle of God's love in Campbell's theology is demonstrated in the pages that follow. The title of this book, a phrase from Campbell's *The Nature of the Atonement*, refers to the central role of the love of God and its nature in extending itself to human persons.

Campbell was a product of a devout Scottish Calvinist home, located in a century characterized by conflict and division within the Church of Scotland as well as momentous changes in theological thinking on the Continent, in Britain and in America. Thus, although his theological writings bear important similarities to John Calvin and explicitly claim connection with Jonathan Edwards, they also demonstrate the influences which can be seen in the work of other nineteenth century theologians like Horace Bushnell, Albrecht Ritschl and Friedrich Schleiermacher.[8] Because of Campbell's unique position both as an inheritor of the Reformed tradition and as an exemplar of some of the nineteenth century's characteristics emphases, Campbell's atonement theology presents a unique opportunity. It is an opportunity to evaluate and test a theory which preserves the best features of traditional atonement accounts, that is, attention to the objective aspects of atonement, as well as the best features of typical nineteenth century accounts, namely, much stronger attention to the subjective aspect of the atonement, the affective, moral, or spiritual change in the human believer.

It is precisely this balance of approach which can bridge theories otherwise thought to be adverse that distinguishes and recommends

Campbell for consideration in today's theological climate. Because of the remarkably inclusive, fair, non-defensive and balanced nature of Campbell's atonement theory, he has something to contribute to today's discussion and we have something to gain from him. Campbell certainly deserves a hearing on the considerable intrinsic merits of his atonement theology, but he has earned, I think, an extra share of attentive consideration by the generosity and openness of *The Nature of the Atonement*, a generosity and openness all the more remarkable when one considers the fact that he was deposed in 1831 from the ordained ministry of the Church of Scotland for supposed heretical views on atonement issues.

This book consists of five chapters. The first gives an account of the life and ministry of John McLeod Campbell, with attention to the influences on his work and the context of his day. The second chapter explicates and critiques the rather complex atonement theology of Campbell, paying attention as well to issues such as methodology and presuppositions.

The third chapter examines the nature and function of atonement typologies. The relevance of this investigation for a study of Campbell is clear when it is noted that Campbell's theory is frequently either rejected or warmly embraced on the basis of a claim that it is either objective or subjective. This is, in part, a typology claim. But, too often, such a claim goes unsupported. Chapter three will lay out what is at stake in the classification of atonement theories.

Part of the task of chapter three is to demonstrate the balance of objective and subjective elements in Campbell's atonement theology. Far from a mere subjective or moral influence theory, Campbell's atonement theology is primarily an objective account with immediate and impressive subjective implications. The balance of these objective and subjective aspects is a strength of Campbell's account. These aspects will be articulated and demonstrated in this study.

Chapter four will look more carefully at some of the important issues only briefly noted in chapter two and some of the difficulties of Campbell's atonement theology noted by his interpreters. It will be claimed that the apparent problems in Campbell's atonement theology are not ultimately insuperable and, in most cases, are solved by greater attention to the focus of Campbell's atonement theology on the desire of divine love. It will also be demonstrated that Campbell's idiosyncratic terminology reveals a theology of remarkable energy, application, and vision.

Chapter five will take up the question of continuity between Campbell and Calvin. The issue of whether Campbell returned to or deviated from the tradition of Calvin is a major interpretive question which arises in a critical analysis of *The Nature of the Atonement*. In Campbell's own context, the particular emphases of Federal Calvinism dominated the Church of Scotland. The primary impetus of Campbell's theology is in response to and reaction against these Federalist emphases, especially as they impacted theories of the atonement. Campbell was convinced that the tradition of the early Reformers had gone astray in the writings of the Calvinists. However explicitly Campbell distanced his own theology from the Calvinists, the question yet emerges on the connections and continuities between the atonement theology of Campbell and the atonement reflections of John Calvin.

Chapter five, then, will make the case that Campbell's atonement theology stands in significant and striking continuity with important themes in John Calvin. This marks Campbell as a significant voice in the Reformed tradition, one who employs metaphors for the atonement not traditionally associated with the Reformed tradition. What will emerge in Campbell's atonement theology is a significant and promising option for those who wish to maintain continuity with the Reformed tradition but yet are compelled to address some of the tradition's most entrenched problems.

In effect, Campbell accomplished two things in *The Nature of the Atonement*. First, he reclaimed some specific, and important, Calvinian themes that had been muted or bypassed in the centuries following Calvin. Second, he enlarged or broadened the tradition of Calvinism by his own unique insights and contributions to theological reflection.

Specifically, Campbell's views on the sacrifice of Christ and the believer's participation in the state of reconciliation, although viewed by some to be avant-garde or wholly unpromising, are central elements in Campbell's theory, a theory which not only captures the essential features of a Reformed doctrine of the atonement but offers several splendid nuances and insights as well. What is surprising, and commonly missed among some Campbell interpreters, is that these nuances and insights are not frivolous innovations, and certainly not heretical, but rather indicate a basic fidelity to the original genius of the Reformed tradition and a display of its breadth, diversity and dynamic character.

Furthermore, Campbell's atonement theology is well-integrated with other central Christian doctrines; his views of the relationships between Christ and the Father or between Christ and the believer, for instance, importantly affect related doctrines such as the doctrine of the Trinity, the doctrine of the Holy Spirit, and the doctrine of the continual intercession of Christ before the Father.

This study is timely for theologians today who are attempting to explicate and articulate atonement doctrine. An investigation of Campbell's compelling atonement reflections can inform, inspire, guide, and instruct theologians who are concerned with the doctrine of the atonement in the context of modernity. It is an atonement theology rich with dynamic, relational imagery, with visionary integration between the historic event and the present experience of salvation, and by a broad Christian vision of God's outstretched love and a responding human community.

NOTES

1. Examples of these kinds of atonement reflections are: Rita Nakashima Brock, *Journeys by Heart: A Christology of Erotic Power* (New York: Crossroad Publishing Company, 1988); Paul M. van Buren, *A Theology of the Jewish Christian Reality: Christ in Context* (San Francisco: Harper & Row, 1988).

2. For instance, Leonardo Boff, *Passion of Christ, Passion of the World: The Facts, their Interpretation, and their Meaning Yesterday and Today*, trans. Robert R. Barr (Maryknoll, New York: Orbis Books, 1987).

6

3. These include: Colin Gunton, *The Actuality of Atonement: A Study of Metaphor, Rationality, and the Christian Tradition* (Grand Rapids, MI: Eerdmans, 1989); Ronald J. Feenstra and Cornelius Plantinga, Jr., eds. *Trinity, Incarnation, and Atonement: Philosophical and Theological Essays* (Notre Dame: University of Notre Dame Press, 1989); Richard Swinburne, *Responsibility and Atonement* (Oxford: Clarendon Press, 1989); Paul Fiddes, *Past Event and Present Salvation: The Christian Idea of Atonement* (Louisville: Westminster/John Knox Press, 1989).

4. A few of the Scottish and British theologians who express direct debt to and appreciation of Campbell include Robert W. Dale, J. Scott Lidgett, John Caird, Edward Caird, R.C. Moberly, James Denney, P.T. Forsyth, George Hendry, and Colin Gunton.

5. For examples of the generally negative critique of Campbell by orthodox or traditional evangelical theologians, see Benjamin Breckinridge Warfield, *The Person and Work of Christ* (Philadelphia: The Presbyterian and Reformed Publishing Company, 1950), pp. 367-368, where he says in reference to Campbell's theory and others like it, "Such theories, while preserving the sacrificial form of the Biblical doctrine . . . fall so far short of the Biblical doctrine of the nature and effect of Christ's sacrifice as to seem little less than travesties of it"; Robert S. Franks, *The Atonement* (Oxford: Oxford University Press, 1934), p. 184, rejects Campbell's theory which includes the novel element of vicarious repentance because, ". . . God *demands* vicarious suffering of some sort from Christ, before He can rightly forgive sin"; John R. W. Stott, *The Cross of Christ* (Downers Grove, Illinois: InterVarsity Press, 1986), p. 141, classifies Campbell's atonement theology as one of the "ingenious attempts to retain language of substitution while rejecting penal aspects," an attempt he deplores; and the *New Dictionary of Theology*, ed. Sinclair B. Ferguson and David Wright (Downers Grove, Illinois: Intervarsity Press, 1988), pp. 126-127, takes a critical, reductionist view of Campbell. Other examples include late near-contemporaries of Campbell, such as A.B. Bruce in *The Humiliation of Christ* (Edinburgh: T & T Clark, 1895), p. 318, where he pronounces Campbell's theory "something very like absurdity."

6. Eugene Garrett Bewkes, *Legacy of a Christian Mind* (Philadelphia: Judson Press, 1937). Also, Thomas H. Hughes, *The Atonement: Modern Theories of the Doctrine* (London: George Allen & Unwin, Ltd., 1949), p. 140, identifies Campbell as an "ethical satisfaction" theorist.

7. There has been significant positive critique of Campbell by a wide variety of interpreters. See Trevor A. Hart, "Anselm of Canterbury and John McLeod Campbell: Where Opposites Meet?", *The Evangelical Quarterly* 62 (1990), 311-333, an article which finds strong continuity between Anselm and Campbell; Brian Gerrish's very fine chapter on Campbell in *Tradition and the Modern World; Reformed Theology in the Nineteenth Century* (Chicago: The University of Chicago Press, 1978), pp. 71-98, which makes a strong case for the continuity of Campbell with Calvin as well as continuity with important themes of the nineteenth century; John Macquarrie's generally positive review in "John McLeod Campbell, 1800-72," *The Expository Times* 83 (1972), 263-268; James B. Torrance, "The Contribution of McLeod Campbell to Scottish Theology," *Scottish Journal of Theology* 26 (1973), 295-311, a very appreciative assessment of Campbell. Both James Torrance and Thomas F. Torrance are enthusiastic admirers of Campbell. See also George Tuttle, *So Rich a Soil; John McLeod Campbell on Christian Atonement* (Edinburgh: Handsel Press, 1986), Christian Kettler's 1987 Ph.D. dissertation on Campbell from Fuller Theological Seminary, *The Vicarious Humanity of Christ and the Reality of Salvation*, and James C. Goodloe's 1987 Ph.D. dissertation from the University of Chicago, *John McLeod Campbell, the Atonement and the Transformation of the Religious Consciousness* - all highly positive accounts of Campbell which claim him in a line of continuity with orthodox theology. This present study differs from the above appreciative accounts of Campbell in several respects. It offers a more complete and detailed critique of Campbell's atonement theology than has previously existed and it makes a case for specific and important lines of continuity between Campbell and Calvin.

Then there are the occasional accounts of Campbell which cross the border from warm appreciation to hagiography. Such glowing regard for Campbell can be seen in N. Brysson Morrison's small book, *They Need No Candle: Builders of Presbyterianism in Scotland 1500-1950* (Richmond: John Knox Press, 1957), 51,52: "Through him thinking men began to regard the fact of the Atonement as greater than any theory of it. Through him theology advanced steadily toward a broader, more tolerant and spiritual expansion. Toward the end of his life he was described as the most completely and profoundly Protestant of living theologians. Today he is called the greatest of all Scottish theologians. Indeed, thinking men believe that to him perhaps more than to any other single mind we owe a spiritual interpretation of the central Christian ideas."

8. Nineteenth century contemporaries or near-contemporaries who influenced Campbell are not easy to identify outside of his own circle of friends and acquaintances. Campbell certainly was aware of some of the changes in theological reflection on the Continent, in Britain, and in

America, but whether he grasped their full import and implications is not clear.

CHAPTER ONE

THE LIFE OF JOHN MCLEOD CAMPBELL

John McLeod Campbell was born in 1800 near Kilninver, in Aryllshire, Scotland, a small village on the west coast of Scotland. He was the first of three children to his parents Dr. Donald Campbell, a minister in the Church of Scotland and Mary McLeod Campbell, who died when John was only six years old. Perhaps because of this early tragedy in their family life, John and his father developed an exceptionally close and intimate relationship.[1]

John's education at the University of Glasgow began when he was eleven years old. Later in life, John confessed to being an idle student, but that hardly seems to be the case. He distinguished himself on several occasions by being awarded prizes in Logic and Moral Philosophy, when he was fifteen and sixteen. After his university course in Glasgow was completed, he entered the Divinity Hall in Glasgow to pursue theological studies and completed this course of study at Edinburgh. Besides the usual prescribed studies, he also demonstrated his interest in other subjects, including Natural History, Political Economy, French, Chemistry, Anatomy, and Mineralogy. He graduated in 1821, at the age of twenty-one.

For the next few years, Campbell continued to study and learn before he felt ready to take on the responsibilities of a parish. He attended lectures in Edinburgh, read widely in Scottish philosophy, and kept a journal of thoughts and ideas. In September, 1825, he was called to the ministry at Row, a parish on the east shore of the Garelock, near Loch Long, in the county of Dunbartonshire, just to the west of Glasgow. There, John struck up a friendship with Robert Story, the minister in the parish on the other side of the lake. Robert Story would be a faithful friend and supporter of Campbell for many years. Campbell met two other friends in 1828 who would prove to be both mentors and friends. The first was Thomas Erskine, a lawyer by profession, but keenly interested in theological matters. He was to have a direct influence on Campbell's views on the nature of the Atonement. Shortly afterward, Campbell met the famous, and controversial, preacher Edward Irving. Irving and Campbell, although different in many important respects theologically, supported each other and, in their infrequent visits, always enjoyed vigorous discussion.

Campbell's few years in the Row parish were filled with relentless activity. He did not spare himself in any of the tasks of his parish, including preaching several times each week, parochial visiting to every home in the parish, diaconal work among the poor, education of the youth, visiting the sick, funerals, presbytery business, as well as assisting neighboring pastors in their duties.

Suspicion and Deposition

Only about a year and a half after he had been ordained at Row, Campbell began to experience resistance to some of his teachings, especially with respect to the doctrine of Assurance. The prevailing doctrine in the Church of Scotland at that time was that true faith must be tested and found acceptable by the presence of "Evidences," namely, virtues or good works that demonstrated faith's genuineness. Campbell saw how burdened and fearful this doctrine made his parishioners. To them, the Gospel had become another Law. John Campbell attempted to dissuade his own congregation, as well as other congregations and his colleagues, from what he perceived to be a dark and dismal view of Christian Assurance. Instead, he began openly preaching a doctrine of Assurance as the very essence of true faith. He expressed this doctrine as one of "resting assured of (God's) love in Christ to them as individuals, and of their individually having eternal life given to them in Christ."[2]

This teaching was perceived by many of his colleagues, and some of his parishioners, as antinomian and they began to view him with some suspicion. One of his parishioners, a Peter MacLeod, remembered that Campbell preached "from the pulpit of Row Church that Christ died for all men. That the sins of every individual were pardoned in consequence of the death of Christ - that all that is necessary for a sinner enjoying Eternal Life is to believe that God so loved him that He gave Christ to die for him, that Christ accordingly did die for him and that therefore his sins are pardoned."[3]

The Session clerk, James Brown, collected a list of things against Campbell as well. Brown solemnly declared that he heard Campbell teach:

1. That God has forgiven every human being his sins past and present and future, whether they believe it or not - the sin of unbelief excepted.
2. That God loves every person alike.
3. That Christ has died for and redeemed everyone in the same sense.
4. That it is a sin to pray for an interest in Christ. Why? Because we have that interest already.
5. That the imputation of Christ's righteousness is a fiction of the devil.
6. That no one is a Christian unless they be positively assured of their own salvation. So much so, that if they were to die the next moment they would be safe.[4]

Yet another parishioner, Mr. Munro, gave an account of the errors of Campbell's preaching:

He has heard Mr. Campbell in his sermons frequently touch on the doctrine of atonement and pardon through the death of Christ - understands him to hold that through the merits of the death of Christ pardon has been extended to the whole human race without exception and without distinction - that the Blessing of Forgiveness was not an offer but a gift put into their possession - that by the death of Christ, all men were in a state of pardon and reconciliation with God - that the atonement of Christ was co-extensive with the sins of all mankind - understands Mr. Campbell to say that the reason why pardon did not result in salvation to any individual was that the individual did not open his eyes to the Son of God or the Gift - Mr. Campbell held that assurance is of the essence of faith and necessary to salvation and witness thinks that in illustration of this subject Mr. Campbell stated that a man must be as conscious of his spiritual state in regard to God as a soldier would be of the act of his passing from the ranks of a rebellious army to those of loyalty.[5]

These excerpts are quoted at length to convey a sense of what aroused the suspicion and anger of a few of Campbell's people. The fact that these "accusations" sound, for the most part, like brief summaries of the gospel to a reader today makes the story even more fascinating and underscores the difference in the theological temper and climate from the Calvinism of Campbell's time to what might be called a "kinder, gentler" Calvinism of today's Reformed churches.[6]

Campbell's concern over the growing dissent in his parish and surrounding parishes appeared in his letters. He wrote to his father, "At home (Row) there is much resistance. . . The Glasgow ministers have all taken alarm. . . You can easily conceive how much, humanly speaking, I need your support just now. . . "[7] He also expressed a sense of foreboding in a letter to his sister, saying, "I have no wish to leave the Church of Scotland," but insisted he was truer to the standards of the Church of Scotland than his opponents and, furthermore, that he was in clear continuity to Luther and Calvin.[8] In spite of increased resistance by fellow-ministers and parishioners, Campbell continued to preach his distinctive doctrine of the Assurance of faith as well as an equally controversial related doctrine of the universality of the atonement. Campbell put the core of his doctrines in a letter to his father when he wrote that "the question about the atonement (is) the question, 'Is God Love?' and the question about assurance (is), 'Will those who know the name of the Lord put their trust in Him?'"[9]

From some of his colleagues and friends Campbell received warm support. His colleague Robert Story from the parish on the other side of the Gareloch stood by him in the growing storm gathering around Campbell. Edward Irving, on a visit to Row from Edinburgh, expressed his support in a conversation with Campbell, which meant a great deal to Campbell, as he recalled later in one of his letters.[10] His father as well was unfailing in loyalty to his son.

Once initial resistance to Campbell's teaching regarding Assurance of faith and the universality of the Atonement began, the events of the next few years seemed slowly to gather momentum to their inevitable and tragic conclusion. That John McLeod Campbell was a sincere and gifted pastor no one denied. But the mood of the Church of Scotland was defensive and suspicious of doctrinal expressions not in accord with the Westminster Confession and its tradition of federal theology. It was this set of circumstances that surrounded John McLeod Campbell and that led ultimately to his heresy trial.[11]

The circumstances of the proceedings against Campbell can be summarized briefly. In March of 1830 a complaint (called a memorial) was filed with the Presbytery of Dumbarton by twelve of Campbell's own parishioners. Another document was filed as well, this one in full support of Campbell, signed by about eighty of his congregants. It stated "undiminished attachment" to Campbell, explaining that,

> Mr. Campbell continued fervently, in season and out of season, to press on his people the necessity of believing the gospel, of resting on the Lord Jesus Christ alone for salvation, of departing from all iniquity, and living in the hope of a blessed immortality; and that these, his labours of love, had not been without much success; and they trusted that nothing would be done by the Presbytery to weaken the hands of so faithful a minister of the gospel.[12]

Unfortunately, the Presbytery refused to receive this document of loyalty and appreciation from the Row church. Instead, they took the memorial document into evidence and appointed a committee of six men to question John Campbell on his doctrine. Campbell, convinced this committee and its mandate was out of order, refused to cooperate. The committee disbanded with the disclaimer that a "free and brotherly conversation" may have bridged the differences between Campbell and his parishioners but now "there is no room for any amicable arrangement."[13]

The matter came up again at the May meeting of the Presbytery of Dumbarton. Then, at the urging of an elder, Mr. Dunlop, the

14

favorable memorial by the eighty was received and read. Elder
Dunlop proved to be an unswerving supporter of Campbell all the
way through this ecclesiastical process. The May Presbytery meeting
contained some interesting procedural moves. For example, the
twelve original memorialists against Campbell were called in to testify
against Campbell. Only three appeared. A long discussion ensued on
if the three could be questioned "in order to ascertain whether or not
they understood what they complained of."[14]   The Presbytery
decided not to question the three memorialists. Their comprehension
of the issues were not deemed relevant.

In July, a committee from the Presbytery visited the Row church
on a Thursday evening to hear Campbell preach. Apparently, two
sentences in Campbell's sermon were especially objectionable and
seen by the committee to be the expression of Campbell's heretical
doctrine. "God loves every child of Adam with a love the measure
of which is to be seen in the agonies of Christ," was the first and,
"The person who knows that Christ died for every child of Adam, is
the person who is in the condition to say to every human being, 'Let
there be peace with you, peace between you and your God,'" was the
second sentence.[15]   On that evidence, the Presbytery recommended
to the complaintants that their memorial be changed to a libel against
their pastor. Campbell was notified of this in the first week in
September and responded in written form at the next meeting of the
Presbytery later that same month. The libel charge read as follows:

"That albeit the doctrine of universal atonement and pardon
through the blood of Christ, as also the doctrine that assurance is
of the essence of faith, and necessary to salvation, are contrary to
the Holy Scriptures, and to the Confession of Faith, approved by
the General Assemblies of the Church of Scotland, and ratified by
law in the year sixteen hundred and ninety; and were moreover
condemned in the year seventeen hundred and twenty, as being
directly opposed to the word of God, and to the Confession of Faith
and Catechisms of the Church of Scotland: Yet true it is and of
verity, that you the said Mr. John McLeod Campbell hold and have
repeatedly promulgated and expressed the foresaid doctrines. . ."[16]

The records of that September Presbytery meeting are remarkably complete and detailed, documenting the comments and speeches of each of the memorialists and other participants. The main complaint against Campbell alleged that he was in direct opposition to the Standards of the Church of Scotland, namely, the Westminster Confession, the Catechism, and the Confession of 1690. It was also declared that Campbell was in opposition to the Scriptures; this however, was decidedly secondary in the Presbytery's reflections. In fact, one of the memorialists, Rev. Gregor, said, "We are far from appealing to the word of God on this ground; it is by the Confession of Faith that we must stand; by it we hold our livings."[17]   Robert Story, also present, vigorously defended his friend and attempted in his speech to get to the theological heart of the matter. He declared, "The question is, has God expressed his love to all his creatures? Is there a man, woman, or child to whom God has not exhibited some kindness?"[18]   He further supported Campbell's views by quoting Calvin and Knox, as well as stating that the humanity of Christ is final proof of God's love for all persons.[19]   In spite of Story's spirited defense of his friend, the Presbytery voted that the libel against Campbell was relevant, that is, they officially declared the views of John McLeod Campbell heretical. Only Robert Story and Elder Dunlop protested the vote.

At this point, the libel began its further ascent up the ladder of ecclesiastical assemblies. The Synod of Glasgow and Ayr heard the case in April, 1831. Robert Story was there and, once again, energetically protested the actions of the Dumbarton Presbytery and tried to demonstrate the accord of John McLeod Campbell's views with the Standards of the Church and Scripture. Campbell himself was there and had the opportunity to speak. His speech was an impressive example of a tactical effort to refute the charges against him employing the very same materials his libellers used, namely, the Standards of the Church of Scotland and prominent Reformers such as Knox and Calvin. Another primary tactical move was an attempt to distance himself from a controversy which rocked the Church of Scotland a century earlier, the Marrow Controversy.[20] Campbell felt the two issues were similar only superficially and that it did his cause

16

an injustice to find precedent in the case of the Marrowmen. Campbell's speech was incredibly long, covering sixty pages of dense typescript in the record of the case.[21] That the members of the Synod apparently sat through this speech which surely took hours to deliver is one of the more astonishing parts of this very astonishing story.[22]

In spite of many hours of painstaking deliberations the Synod of Glasgow and Ayr was not able to come to a conclusion. Thus, they referred the entire matter to the next meeting of the General Assembly, the highest governing body in the Church of Scotland. The manner in which the General Assembly heard the case against John McLeod Campbell is nothing short of farcical. The debate began, following a full day of attending to other business, after midnight on Tuesday the 24th of May, 1831 and droned on all night. Campbell himself was not given the opportunity to speak. A last minute letter from 420 members of the Row church declaring their regard for their pastor's zeal and piety did not seem to change the mood of the delegates. Documents and evidence totalling several hundreds of pages were not studied by the delegates. Most of them left during the course of the night; out of 310 delegates, only 125 actually voted at 6:15 a.m. the following morning. By a vote of 119 to 6, Campbell was deposed from the Church of Scotland.[23]

Dr. Donald Campbell, John's father, was one of the delegates at that General Assembly of 1831. He gave a speech in defense of his son which demonstrates his utter confidence in him, "Moderator, I am not afraid for my son; though his brethren cast him out, the Master whom he serves will not forsake him; and while I live, I will never be ashamed to be the father of so holy and blameless a son." He added, no doubt with pride and affection as well as sorrow, "Indeed sir, in this respect, I challenge any one in this house to bring forward any who can come into competition with him."[24]

Another anecdote, often told in accounts of Campbell's deposition, ironically illustrates the nature of this Assembly. After the vote of deposition, the principal clerk solemnly uttered his conclusion, but inadvertently reversed the phrases, saying that, "these doctrines of Mr. Campbell would remain and flourish long after the Church of

Scotland had perished and was forgotten." Thomas Erskine, an observer to the proceedings, turned and whispered loudly to his neighbors, "This spake he not of himself, but being High Priest, he prophesied."[25]

Contextual Factors in Campbell's Deposition

Crucial in understanding the events of Campbell's deposition in 1831 is an account of some of the contextual features of the life of this pastor/theologian. These features are, of course, numerous. They include the political pressures in the Church of Scotland in the late eighteenth and early nineteenth centuries, the explosive population growth of Scotland during these years, the impact of the Industrial Revolution and the Enlightenment on the Scottish people, the influence of the American Revolution and the resulting increased exchange between America and Scotland, as well as many others, from pew rents in parish churches to the notoriously difficult question in Scottish church history of lay patronage, an issue which had to do with the procedures for choosing a parish minister.[26] Some of the most influential of the contextual factors surrounding the ministry and deposition of Campbell will be briefly surveyed.

Behind all the disputes and divisions of the late eighteenth and early nineteenth centuries in the Church of Scotland was the rivalry of its two main parties, the Moderates and the Evangelicals, also called the Popular party. Although the nature of these two parties is frequently characterized as liberal against conservative, upper-class against middle and lower-class, educated against common, there is considerable more complexity in the traits of the two parties than these simple designations indicate.

The Moderate Party was the party of power and position in the late eighteenth and early nineteenth centuries. Its intellectual origin can be traced back to the rise of Rationalism in the late seventeenth century. Moderatism in its prime was an intellectual and cultural attitude that supported and reinforced the Scottish Enlightenment and displayed many Enlightenment values such as "genteel manners, religious moderation and tolerance, and high esteem for scientific and literary accomplishments."[27] In addition the leaders of the Moderate party "envisaged a polite Presbyterian clergy overturning the persistent stereotype of Scottish Presbyterian ministers as ignorant, bigoted, and narrow-minded fanatics while guiding Scotland toward virtue, order, and enlightenment."[28] The Moderates contributed impressively to the Scottish Enlightenment, that splendid outpouring of philosophy, science, political theory, church leadership and rhetoric, literature, and poetry in eighteenth century Scotland represented by people like David Hume, William Robertson, Adam Smith, Robert Burns, James Boswell, and James Watt.[29]

The character of the Scottish Enlightenment is distinct from that of the Continental Enlightenment and thus warrants further description. A major feature of the Scottish Enlightenment is its relationship between church and secular culture. In Scotland, the established church came to terms with the Enlightenment and embraced it. This is in significant contrast to the Enlightenment in France where the gap between the established church and the *philosophes* was an intellectual and temperamental chasm.[30] Richard Sher says of the Scottish Enlightenment, "There was no need to astound the world in the manner of a Rousseau or d'Holbach. Nor was it necessary to conceal one's true meaning in the manner of a Voltaire or Diderot. Rather, the dominant tone in Scotland was one of straightforward didacticism - a tone better suited to pulpit and classroom oratory than to subtle exotic tales, witty social satires, or irreverent attacks on accepted values and established institutions."[31]

The Scottish Enlightenment in late eighteenth century was distinct in several other important ways. For one, it was the ideology of "self-satisfied Scottish Presbyterian ministers seeking to promulgate humane, enlightened principles without altering in any significant way the existing structure of religious, social and political institutions."[32] It was, in short, a politically and socially conservative attitude, one not much interested in examining social structures and economic hardships of the rapidly expanding population in urban centers in Scotland.[33]

Some of the features of the Scottish Enlightenment parallel that of the Continent. Its emphasis on spreading morality, virtue, polite and genteel manners, the rational capacities of the human mind, and a resistance to religious intolerance were shared by Enlightenment thinkers across the Channel.

The character of the Moderate party at the peak of its influence and importance reveals one important underlying tension. There was a tension between the Moderate party's liberal views on theological matters, religious tolerance, and intellectual freedom on the one hand and its more conservative views on social, political, and ecclesiastical law and order, hierarchy and subordination on the other hand.[34] Thus, for example, the Moderates were quick to support the controversial Roman Catholic relief of 1778, an issue of religious tolerance, but had no sympathy for the American colonists in their struggle for political independence.

It was about the time of John McLeod Campbell's birth in 1800 that the power and prestige of the Moderate party began to decline in the Church of Scotland. The particular Enlightenment values of the Moderates were dying out, to be replaced by the more characteristic nineteenth century characteristics such as romanticism, political independence, and social equality as well as the powerful and pervasive influence of evangelicalism.[35]

It was the Popular party, or Evangelicals, a group long active but less powerful in the Church of Scotland, that emerged at the turn of the century as the church's dominant, but divisive, force. Evangelical leaders tended to solve their difficulties with the Church of Scotland by means of secession. Patronage was always one of the primary sources of friction between the Evangelicals and the Moderates, leading to several secessions by the year 1800 as well as the Disruption of 1843 from which emerged the Free Church of Scotland, led by Thomas Chalmers.

In temperament, the Evangelicals differed from the Moderates. In contrast to the theological liberalism of the Moderates, the Evangelicals were theologically conservative, although also convinced of the primary importance of the personal relationship between the believer and God. In contrast to the political and ecclesiastical conservatism of the Moderates, the Evangelicals were political and ecclesiastical radicals, supporting the American colonists in their struggle for independence and repudiating the idea of the state

Church.[36] In contrast to the social conservatism of the Moderates, the Evangelicals were deeply committed to social welfare programs, Sunday School outreach programs, and mission.[37]

It was against this background of declining Moderate influence and increasing Evangelical influence that Campbell's heresy trial in 1831 was set. However, it is not easy to see just how those old party rivalries played themselves out in the case of Campbell.[38] Campbell does not fit easily into the Moderate party with their profile of genteel Enlightenment values but neither does he fit well the picture of the Evangelical, so determinedly committed to the letter of the Westminster Confession. Campbell seems to be a hybrid mix of certain characteristics of both parties. He fits the theological openness of the Moderates, although that openness in Campbell also has a decidedly un-Moderate emphasis on the heart's relation to a personal, loving God. He fits the profile of the Evangelical with respect to interest in social welfare, mission, and piety but he also explicitly distances himself from standard Evangelical Calvinist orthodoxy.

Perhaps because Campbell had no clear party loyalties, he received no significant support from either side during the hearing at the General Assembly in 1831. Aside from several earnest and moving testimonies from close friends and his own father, Campbell had not built up any party support or an assured block of votes. In addition, because of the eclectic, independent nature of his thinking and preaching, both Moderates and Evangelicals could and did find something to object to. The fact that the vote was overwhelmingly against him illustrates his solitary position in the Church of Scotland at that time.

Another important contextual factor in understanding the Campbell deposition is the link that was frequently made between the Campbell case and the notorious Marrow controversy of the early eighteenth century. The Marrow controversy is traced back to the book, *The Marrow of Modern Divinity*, published in London in 1645, most likely by Edward Fisher. The Westminster Assembly was in session at this time and the book received the official endorsement of the censor of theological books acting under the authority of the

Westminster Assembly. The book, thus approved, retreated into obscurity for more than fifty years. But when it reappeared in the context of a heresy trial of a minister accused of antinomian errors at the General Assembly in 1717, the book itself was brought under suspicion of antinomianism and was officially censored by the General Assembly in 1720. Twelve ministers, called "The Marrowmen," petitioned the Assembly in 1721 to revoke the condemnation, thus bringing themselves under suspicion as well. In 1722, the Act of 1720 was confirmed, the Marrow doctrine prohibited, and the twelve ministers rebuked.

The complete, and complex, story of the Marrow controversy cannot be told here. It is interesting that the account of the Marrow controversy has been given as wide a range of interpretation as the Campbell heresy story. For instance, some authors see a neat division between the "religious Calvinism" of the Marrowmen and the "logical Calvinism" of the General Assembly.[39] But other authors feel the issues have not yet been carefully analyzed and that the picture is considerably more complex.[40]

At a very general level, there is similarity between the Marrow controversy and the Campbell controversy. Both the Marrowmen and John McLeod Campbell were interested in articulating a theological system founded on the love of God and the experience of salvation rather than a theological system founded on logical reflection on the decrees of God. But there are also numerous important differences between the two controversies which should not be blurred.

The fact that the opponents of Campbell felt they could label him with the supposed disrepute of the Marrowmen illustrates, perhaps paradoxically, both the lack of accurate perception of the particulars of Campbell's theology as well as some foundational similarity of the two cases. The mere fact that the two cases are frequently compared illustrates the persistent ambivalence in Scottish Calvinism, from the early 1700s to at least the mid-1800s over central theological issues such as the assurance of faith, the extent of the atonement, and relationship between gospel and law in the Christian life.

Publication of The Nature of the Atonement

After John McLeod Campbell was removed from the Row parish, he organized an independent congregation in Glasgow where he ministered for many years. He wrote several theological books: a book on the Lord's Supper, *Christ the Bread of Life* in 1851; his most important book, *The Nature of the Atonement and its Relation to Remission of Sins and Eternal Life* in 1856; and a final book on revelation, *Thoughts on Revelation* in 1862.

Although Campbell's deposition from the ministry of the Church of Scotland was effected in part because of supposed heretical views with respect to the *extent* of the atonement, it gradually became clear to Campbell that the real issue had to do with the *nature* of the Atonement. In the mid-1840s his letters began to contain repeated reflections on the nature of the atonement.[41] His book, *The Nature of the Atonement* appeared in 1856 as a result of these reflections which fundamentally challenged the accepted doctrine in the Church of Scotland at that time.

A first exposure to Campbell's book on the atonement is a daunting experience. His style is difficult, with very long sentences of multiple clauses. Quotes from other authors are scarce; when they do exist, there is no citation. Often the argument wanders into related issues; at times a great deal is made of very little and at other times one wishes a really crucial idea was given more space to expand and grow. There are peculiarities of organization and frequent repetition. Most interpreters of Campbell cited so far in this study complain about his style and congratulate the reader who perseveres through the nearly four hundred pages of paragraph-length sentences in *The Nature of the Atonement*. But the book, although characterized by a difficult style, is not hard to understand. Especially if one has grown accustomed to Campbell's personality by a familiarity with his letters and sermons, the cadence of the book becomes more pleasing and the thesis clearer.

The book was received with mixed reviews. A review of the March 8, 1856 *Literary Churchman* was critical of the book in that it did not exhibit adequate knowledge of the Church Fathers. In a letter to his publisher, Campbell acknowledged that point, noting, "I cannot doubt that such an acquaintance with the Fathers as some enjoy would have enabled me to engraft my book on the past with some advantages." But he adds that perhaps the lack of scholarly paraphernalia was just as well: ". . . even had I had the necessary qualification in respect of reading, it would have interfered with the simplicity of my aim to have availed myself of it."[42] Another critical review appeared that same year, in the *National Review*. The reviewer, James Martineau, an influential British Unitarian, had several specific complaints concerning the book, specifically, on Campbell's concept of the relationship between Christ and the believer and Campbell's unique view of the confession of Christ.[43] Campbell deemed Martineau's review important enough to respond to it at some length in an appendix to the second edition of *The Nature of the Atonement*.

An appreciative review by Constantine Prichard, Rector of South Luffenham, appeared after the publication of the second edition in 1867. Campbell was pleased with this review and corresponded with Mr. Pritchard on some details of the book's argument.[44]

Because the book was published by a London company and because Campbell had a number of friends in London, the book circulated both in the Scottish and English churches. The influence of *The Nature of the Atonement* has been continuous in Scotland and England from its publication to the present.[45]

Later Life, Friendships and Influences, and Death

John McLeod Campbell married Mary Campbell in 1838, at the age of thirty-eight. Six children were born to them, four sons (one of whom died in infancy) and two daughters. The details of Campbell's life after his deposition need not be recounted here in full. The evidence of his own *Reminiscences* and the *Memorials*, which his son Donald Campbell compiled, give the picture of a man with a wide variety of commitments and constant demands on his time. His schedule was often brutal, much to the concern of his friends and his family. At times, his health broke down completely and he was compelled to rest for a period of months or even years.[46] When he was well, Campbell travelled often. He was frequently in England

and also enjoyed several extended visits in Europe with friends such as Thomas Chalmers, Thomas Erskine, Robert Story, and his brother Donald Campbell.

The friends of Campbell and the natural influences they exerted on his theological development is an important element in understanding Campbell's theology. It is clear from his letters that he invested in his friends and family much personal energy and commitment. What is especially interesting about Campbell's friends is their diversity on theological questions yet their loyalty to Campbell. The circle included Edward Irving and F.D. Maurice, both of whom he had fundamental disagreements with as well as Thomas Chalmers, Thomas Erskine, Robert Story, Norman McLeod and A.J. Scott with whom he shared closer theological convictions.

The most famous name of the group of Campbell's friends is F.D. Maurice, a thinker of wide interest and influence in the Church of England during the nineteenth century. Maurice published books and articles on many subjects, including history of philosophy, theology, and ethics and was passionately interested in the responsibility of the Church for social reform. Campbell met Maurice in London in 1838 and, although they visited together only infrequently over the years, became good friends.[47] Maurice knew of Campbell and had read his sermons before the two men met. Both shared significant similarities not only in theological approaches but also in experiences of official resistance from their respective churches.[48]

Maurice acknowledged the influence of Campbell on his own thought and, in fact, it seems that Campbell influenced Maurice more than the other way around.[49] As for Campbell, he was sometimes skeptical of Maurice's theological ideas but he was, characteristically, willing to withhold judgement, trusting Maurice's character and basic instincts.[50]

Thomas Erskine was a life-long friend, ardent supporter and significant influence on Campbell as well. Erskine was not a theologian by profession but by avocation. Trained as an attorney, he retired from the legal profession and took up a life of study, made possible by a his possession of a large inheritance. Erskine had a remarkable mind and, although his knowledge of the history of dogma was limited, his spirituality, theological insights, and loyalty profoundly affected not only Campbell, but F.D. Maurice as well. Both Campbell and Maurice, as effusively evidenced by their letters, were bound to Thomas Erskine by a singular bond of friendship and affection.[51]

Erskine published several important books long before Campbell's heresy trail and book on the atonement appeared.[52] They met sometime at the beginning of Campbell's parish ministry at Row. But, although the two thinkers shared strong similarities in their theological formulations, it is better said that they were companions rather than master and student.[53] Erskine's name does not appear at all in Campbell's *The Nature of the Atonement* but in a letter to his friend, Campbell said that, ". . . in writing it you were mentally present with me . . . as one on whose sympathy I could calculate."[54] On other issues, Campbell disagreed with Erskine and, although he did not publicize these differences, admitted them to acquaintances.[55]

Edward Irving is another of Campbell's friends who claims a certain fame, or, perhaps, infamy, in the history of the Church of Scotland. Irving too was deposed from the ministry of the Church of Scotland. In fact, the same 1831 General Assembly that deposed Campbell began initial proceedings against Irving and his Presbytery deposed him officially in 1833. He died just a year later. Irving began his ministry in Glasgow as an assistant to Thomas Chalmers, then took a church in London, and finished his career in Edinburgh.[56] Irving is best known for his powerful preaching and the vigorous pentecostal expressions of worship which swept through his church. For this, in part, he was regarded with great suspicion.[57] It is difficult to know just what did happen in worship services in Irving's church, but according to many reports, considerable confusion ensued. One otherwise sympathetic interpreter of Irving said that "disorder reigned in Irving's church, and scenes of wild excitement were witnessed week by week . . . The screams and gesticulations of frenzied men and women. . . filled Irving's best friends with sorrow and even shame."[58] In addition, Irving's Christology, built on the conviction of Christ's absolute identification with sinful humanity,

26

allowed for the possibility of sin in Christ.[59]   This, ultimately, was considered heretical by the General Assembly in 1831 and Irving was deposed by the Presbytery of Annan in 1833.

Campbell and Irving knew each other only five years before Irving's death in 1834. Yet, the two men clearly impacted one another's theological formulations and both shared significant theological assumptions. Both were utterly convinced that true religion was heart religion, that assurance of God's will to save was an integral part of faith and that God's primary posture toward humanity was love and forgiveness. In one significant conversation in 1828, Campbell expounded his developing thought regarding the love of God to Irving. He reports in a letter, "Irving listened to me with that earnest weighing attention which was characteristic of him. He then got up and paced back and forward for a good while, during which I was silent. At last he stopped and said, 'I believe you are right, and that you were sent to show me this.' . . .From that time he preached the Atonement as for all. . ."[60]

The influence of Campbell's family, close friends and acquaintances both on his personal life and his theological work is without dispute.   He himself acknowledges his debt to Erskine, Irving, Chalmers, Story, Maurice, and many others repeatedly in his correspondence. What is not as clear are possible nineteenth century contemporaries or near-contemporaries who influenced Campbell. Campbell's habit in his correspondence to his family and friends was to deal primarily with personal matters, local and national church issues, and reflections on specific problems in theology. In addition, he was liberal with advice, sympathy and pastoral concern. Campbell's habit in his theological writings was to cite sources only very rarely and then, usually, from a lesser known Scottish or British divine. Thus, there is very little evidence on the question of broader nineteenth century influences on Campbell's theology.

It is almost certain that Campbell did not read German, so Schleiermacher's direct influence becomes doubtful, as the English translation of his important works did not appear until after Campbell's death.[61] However, by the mid-1860s, more than ten years after the publication of *The Nature of the Atonement*, Campbell was certainly aware of Schleiermacher's importance and offered some brief critical evaluation of Schleiermacher. In a letter to his oldest son just a few years before his death, Campbell reported that he had just finished reading Schleiermacher's biography. He includes a few brief reactions, saying that the book "has made me acquainted with a new phase of the German mind, as social rather than as absorbed in abstract thought; although a social existence of which self-consciousness and much mental analysis has been the character."[62] Campbell noted the positive influences of Schlei- ermacher's Moravian training but lamented that other concerns had occupied Schleiermacher and he had perhaps forgotten the love of God which calls to him as God's own child. This cryptic criticism of Schleiermacher is fascinating; Campbell is suggesting that this theologian known for his focus on the heart's relationship of utter dependence on God is actually not centered enough on the heart's desire for God.[63] Unfortunately, this letter is the sum total of Campbell's reflections on Schleiermacher and, as such, they appear a full decade after Campbell's book on the atonement.

Albrecht Ritschl, of course, did not become influential until later in the century, again, after Campbell's death. Campbell may have known of Horace Bushnell, although Bushnell's important writings on the atonement appeared after Campbell's book was published.[64] But, although the influences of the momentous theological changes in the nineteenth century cannot be specified exactly, Campbell's writings do exhibit some of the characteristic theological emphases or perspectives of the century. These characteristics include an interest in the moral and spiritual aspects of religion, a turn to ethical inwardness and an emphasis on the truth of direct religious experience.[65]

There were, of course, many other important influences in Campbell's life which inevitably impacted his theological views. These included friends mentioned above such as his colleague Robert Story, his wife Mary and his five surviving children, the deaths of friends and family members over which he deeply mourned, the experiences of several long visits to the Continent and observation of religious practices there, and innumerable other personal influences which can scarcely be documented here. Campbell's life was full and rich, but characterized as well by conflict and grief, pressures and demands, failures and disappointment. In times of exhaustion and sorrow, he experienced the kind of despair and doubt chronicled by Christian believers in all times. Principal Shairp, in his memorial letter to Campbell's son after Campbell's death remembered,

> He mentioned that once in recent years, after the death of his brother, when his own whole body and mind were very much shattered, he found all the scaffolding of thoughts and arguments, which he had laboriously built up, fall away, and there was no help in them. What he might have offered to others at a like time, were then wholly unavailing for himself. One thing only was helpful, (and this, he said, was a precious lesson to him,) he had to begin at the old beginning - he had to be just like a child, to believe, to put forth simple faith, where he could see nothing, to roll himself over upon God. And this, I think he said, brought comfort when nothing else did.[66]

John McLeod Campbell died in 1872 after a brief illness. His funeral was held in Robert Story's church in Rosneath, just across the lake from his first church of Row and the scene of all the controversy forty years earlier. His son Donald describes the funeral as an event "attended by a large company" of people from his congregation in Glasgow, former parishioners in Row, as well as many Church of Scotland ministers. Robert Story and Norman McLeod preached the funeral sermons; their eulogies excelled in warmest regard, respect and affection for their life-long friend and companion. Norman McLeod said about Campbell, "His character was the most perfect embodiment I have ever seen of the character of Jesus Christ . . ."[67] Robert Story said, "He had fought a good fight, he had finished his course, he had kept the faith; and he found here, close to the unforgotten scenes of his early ministry and early troubles, the haven of his repose."[68]

Letters of testimony also give witness to the character, intellect and influence of this remarkable man. One of Campbell's friends,

Canon D.J. Vaughan, wrote a letter of gratitude, affection, and respect to Campbell's eldest son, Donald Campbell. Its words give a fitting conclusion to this survey of the life and ministry of John McLeod Campbell. "The first impression was of transparent simplicity, candor, and goodness - a nature most truthful and lovable and trustworthy. I remember perfectly on that first visit, as always afterwards, how careful he was to do full justice to views not exactly in accordance with his own . . . And never once did I trace in him the slightest wish for victory in argument, or for the triumph of anything but simple truth and right."[69]

NOTES

1. Much of the material for this brief overview of John McLeod Campbell's life comes from a two-volume set of his letters, collected and edited by his son, Donald Campbell, after John's death. Cf. *Memorials of John McLeod Campbell, D.D.; Being Selections from his Correspondence* (London: Macmillan & Co., 1877).

2. Memorials, Vol. 1, p. 50.

3. Iain B. Galbraith, *A Village Heritage* (Rhu and Shandon Kirk Session publication, 1981), p. 40. This small book was published by the Parish of Rhu in celebration of their organ centenary. It contains a history of the parish, as well as a history of the organ. The book reports the discovery of some old parish documents in a box in the tower room of the church just the previous year, in 1980. One of these documents, dated 1831, is titled, "Precognitions of Witnesses for the Libellers in the case against Mr. Campbell." This quote, and the few that follow, are taken from this old document. It is a first hand account of what some of Campbell's parishioners found objectionable to his teaching.

4. Galbraith, *A Village Heritage*, p. 41.

5. *A Village Heritage*, p. 43,44.

6. This phrase comes from the title of an article by Richard Mouw in the *Reformed Journal* 40 (Oct. 90), 11-13.

30

7. *Memorials*, Vol. 1, pp. 46-47.

8. *Memorials*, Vol. 1, p. 64.

9. *Memorials*, Vol. 1, p. 109.

10. *Memorials*, Vol. 1, p. 54.

11. The full account of the charges brought against Campbell and his eventual dismissal from the Church of Scotland have been recorded in several places, including a biography of Robert Story by his son, a volume of Campbell's own memories of the heresy trial, *Reminiscences and Reflections*, and a complete record of the presbytery and synod actions against Campbell, *The Whole Proceedings Before the Presbytery of Dumbarton, and Synod of Glasgow and Ayr in the case of the Rev. John McLeod Campbell* (Greenock: R.B. Lusk, 1831). Edward Irving was also brought up for church discipline at the 1831 General Assembly that deposed Campbell, but the action against him was not completed until 1833.

12. *Whole Proceedings*, p. vii.

13. *Whole Proceedings*, p. ix.

14. *Whole Proceedings*, p. xiii.

15. *Whole Proceedings*, p. xix,xx.

16. *Memorials*, vol. 1, p. 70; *Whole Proceedings*, p. 180.

17. *Whole Proceedings*, p. xxix.

18. *Whole Proceedings*, p. xxxi.

19. *Whole Proceedings*, p. xxxii.

20. The issues of the Marrow controversy will be discussed below. Cf. pp. 21,22.

21. *Whole Proceedings*, pp. 174-233.

22. Even the spectators in the gallery listened carefully. At one point in Campbell's speech, hissing broke out in the gallery, apparently in response to a delegate who wished to cut Campbell's speech short. The Moderator

had to sternly warn the spectators to behave or be expelled. Cf. *Whole Proceedings*, pp. 226, 227.

23. Although not much is known about the individual delegates to the General Assembly of 1831 besides the names of those who gave speeches, there are some general observations that can be made. The delegates were comprised of ministers and elders. The elders were usually men of property and higher social standing. Although in the parish churches there were occasionally tradesmen and merchants as elders, the General Assembly was predominantly filled by the propertied classes, including baronets, lawyers, judges, and professors. Richard Sher and Alexander Murdoch, "Patronage and Party in the Church of Scotland, 1750-1800," *Church, Politics and Society*, ed. Norman Macdougall (Edinburgh: John Donald Publishers, Ltd., 1983), p. 217, fn. 28.

It is interesting to note that several of the signers of the original memorial against Campbell were tradesmen but the people that ultimately removed him from his office were of the upper class. What specific conclusions, if any, can be drawn from this is far from clear. The point here is simply to note that the General Assembly was in no way representative of the population of the Church of Scotland. This point is utterly obvious when one further notes the all male membership of the General Assembly at that time.

24. *Memorials*, Vol. 1., p. 78.

25. This anecdote is reported widely in literature about Campbell. It comes from a collection of Erskine's letters: William Hanna, ed. *Letters of Thomas Erskine of Linlathen*, 2 vols. (New York: G.P. Putnam's Sons, 1877), Vol. 1, p. 136-7.

26. Lay patronage was one of the most volatile and persistent issues to provoke dissent in the Church of Scotland in the eighteenth and nineteenth centuries. It was a major cause of at least two secessions from the Church of Scotland, the Seceders in 1732 and the Disruption in 1843. The tradition of the Church of Scotland since the Reformation had assigned the responsibility of appointing pastors to the "patron" of the parish, usually a wealthy landowner, the Crown, or the civil authorities. This system aroused much resentment among laypeople and some clergy due to the political and economic power of the patron as well as conflicting notions about proper church government. Hardening rivalries and jealousies in the two major parties in the Church of Scotland, the Moderates and the Popular party, also tended to focus on the patronage issue. Although the patronage issue in particular had little to do with Campbell's deposition in 1831, these party

rivalries were one important factor that led to his dismissal from the ministry. Thus, patronage lurks in the background as one of the key factors of political rivalry which emerged in the Campbell deposition.

The issue of patronage and its role in the secessions of 1732 (Seceders) and 1834 (Disruption) as well as its role in a long list of other ecclesiastical disputes is the subject of extensive research and debate among scholars of Scottish ecclesiastical history. Recently, excellent new work has been done on this question, work which takes into account the broad range of contextual factors. See especially Sher and Murdoch, pp. 214-215.

27. Richard B. Sher, *Church and University in the Scottish Enlightenment; The Moderate Literati of Edinburgh* (Princeton: Princeton University Press, 1985), p. 57.

28. Sher, *Church and University*, p. 57. Another of Sher's designations of the Moderate party is "polite Presbyterianism." Cf. p. 63.

29. Andrew J. Campbell, *Two Centuries of the Church of Scotland, 1707-1929* (Paisley: Alexander Gardner, Ltd., 1930), p. 93. William Robertson was the most important of the Moderate leaders during the peak of Moderate power. His sermons, which clearly articulate Moderate Enlightenment views, were reprinted frequently during the second half of the eighteenth century. This is one indication of how they reflected the dominant mood of Scotland at this time. He said in one sermon, for example, "Christianity not only sanctifies our souls, but refines our man- ner. . ." Cf. *The Situation of the World at the Time of Christ's Appearance, and Its Connexions with the Success of His Religion Considered* (1755), in *The Works of William Robertson*, 2 vols (Edinburgh, 1829), 1:lxxvii-lxxxvi. Quoted in Sher, *Church and University*, p. 63.

30. Sher, *Church and University*, p. 63.

31. Sher, *Church and University*, p. 212.

32. Sher, *Church and University*, p. 211.

33. Glasgow's population more than doubled in the last two decades of the eighteenth century and it doubled again in the first two decades of the nineteenth. Scotland's population as a whole nearly doubled in the first half of the nineteenth century and nearly doubled again in the second half of that century. Much of this explosive growth occurred in large urban centers like Glasgow and Edinburgh as the Industrial Revolution made its mark on Scotland with the emergence of the tobacco industry, cotton mills, iron

works, and other industries. Cf. J.G. Kyd, *Scottish Population Statistics*, Scottish Historical Society, pp. 82-89, quoted in Andrew Drummond and James Bulloch, *The Church in Victorian Scotland, 1843-1874* (Edinburgh: The Saint Andrew Press, 1975), p. 274. See also Andrew Campbell, *Two Centuries of the Church of Scotland*, p. 143 and p. 173.

34. Sher, *Church and University*, p. 262.

35. Sher, *Church and University*, p. 308 and Andrew Campbell, *Two Centuries of the Church of Scotland*, p. 136.

36. Sher, *Church and University*, p. 262.

37. Andrew Campbell, *Two Centuries of the Church of Scotland*, p. 182.

38. George Tuttle, *So Rich a Soil; John McLeod Campbell on Christian Atonement* (Edinburgh: Handsell Press, 1986), p. 35.

39. See Stewart Mechie, "The Marrow Controversy Reviewed," *The Evangelical Quarterly* 22 (January, 1950), p. 28 for a statement of this view.

40. See David C. Lachman, *The Marrow Controversy, 1718-1723* (Edinburgh: Rutherford House Books, 1988), p. 3.

41. Campbell wrote in 1847 to Thomas Erskine, "I have been more than usually with you in spirit of late, having ventured to attempt to teach my people on the subject of the atonement. As respects the *extent* of the atonement - its bearing on the whole human race - the Calvinism of Scotland seems breaking up fast; but this in connection with teaching, which is not light but darkness as to its *nature*; and I feel that the work for this time, if it were so uttered as to command attention, is a word supplying this great want." *Memorials*, Vol. 1, p. 207.

42. *Memorials*, Vol. 1, pp. 273-274.

43. Analysis of this review will be made in chapter four, pp. 121-123.

44. *Memorials*, Vol. 2, pp. 128 and 191. The review by C.E. Pritchard appeared in the *North British Review* 46 (June, 1867).

45. J.H. Leckie perhaps caught the quality of Campbell's influence when he said that Campbell has had a power of "mild persistence" in his impact on subsequent theologians in England and Scotland. From "John McLeod

Campbell's 'The Nature of the Atonement'," *The Expository Times* 40 (1928-1929), p. 203. See also D. Chambers, "Doctrinal Attitudes in the Church of Scotland in the Pre-Disruption Era: the Age of John McLeod Campbell and Edward Irving," *Journal of Religious History* 8 (December 1974), p. 160, "Though he was deposed for heresy, his influence on later British theology has been wide and significant, and some would claim him to be Scotland's greatest theologian." See also Tuttle, chapter 9. Tuttle documents the extensive influence of Campbell on Scottish and British theologians. Among these are J.J. Lias in his 1883-4 Hulsean lectures entitled *The Atonement Viewed in the Light of Modern Difficulties*; John Caird, professor of divinity at Glasgow University and author of *The Fundamental Ideas of Christianity* (1899); R.C. Moberly, professor of pastoral theology at Oxford at the turn of the century and author of an important book often linked with Campbell's, *Atonement and Personality* (1901); Vincent Taylor's important contributions to atonement theology in his reappraisal of the concept of sacrifice also bears clear dependence on Campbell. Taylor's book *Jesus and His Sacrifice* (1955) and Colin Gunton's book *The Actuality of Atonement* (1989) illustrate Campbell's continuing influence throughout this century.

46. One of these times of illness was in 1836, when he was ordered by his doctor to rest undisturbed by work for several months. Again, in 1838, he took several months of rest, travelling to Paris to consult a doctor and living in Paris for the summer with Mr. Erskine. It was that September, shortly after his return from Paris, that Campbell married. Again, in 1843, Campbell moved to a village on the outskirts of Glasgow in the hope of becoming stronger with good country air. In 1849, he was struck with scarlet fever and was gravely ill. A persistent illness forced Campbell to take early retirement from his church in Glasgow in 1858, at the age of 58. These illnesses seemed to result, at least in part, from the exhaustion of interminable pressures and demands of his ministry.

47. *Memorials*, Vol. 1, p. 147.

48. Maurice himself was dismissed from his position as professor of theology at King's College, London for perceived deviations from orthodoxy with respect to eternal punishment and the meaning of eternity. After the dismissal, be became, in 1866, Professor of Moral Philosophy at Cambridge.

49. Tuttle, *So Rich a Soil*, p. 70; Bewkes, *Legacy of a Christian Mind*, p. 8, "It is our opinion that Maurice received far more from the well-springs of Campbell's deeper understanding of the Christian consciousness than he was himself aware."

50. *Memorials*, Vol. 1, p. 255, "I do not feel that I need to be conscious of a full harmony with Maurice in all even that is important in his system, in order to be justified in wishing that he should have a fair hearing. . ." and Vol. 2, p. 12, ". . . I always regard my own misgivings as to him with distrust. . . and so I try to wait, as I may yet see." Also, Vol. 2, p. 343, in a memorial letter from Principal Shairp to Donald Campbell, John McLeod Campbell's oldest son, Principal Shairp remembers several conversations John Campbell had with him regarding the views of Maurice, views which he found particularly troubling. "Then he (Campbell) added, those who like Maurice regard Christ's work as only taking away our alienation, by making us see the Father's eternal good-will toward us, as this only and no more, they take no account of the sense of guilt in man. According to their views, there is nothing real in the nature of things answering to this sense of guilt. The sense of guilt becomes a mistake which further knowledge removes. All sin is thus reduced to ignorance. At another time, when speaking of Christ as the Head of humanity, I understood your father to say that he thought it one of Mr. Maurice's great dangers to carry this so far, as to absorb in it all sense of our own individuality."

51. F.D. Maurice once remarked that Erskine was "the best man I think I ever knew." Cf. Bernard M.G. Reardon, *From Coleridge to Gore, A Century of Religious Thought in Britain* (London: Longman Group Ltd., 1971), p. 398. John and Mary McLeod Campbell named their second infant son after Erskine, calling him Thomas Erksine Campbell. The baby died at six months.

52. These include *Remarks on the Internal Evidence for the Truth of Revealed Religion* (1820), *Essay on Faith* (1822), *The Unconditional Freeness of the Gospel* (1828) and *The Brazen Serpent* (1831).

53. There are contrasting opinions on this issue of the extent of Erskine's influence on Campbell. George Tuttle cites the opposing views in his book on Campbell, p. 67. My own view is that the two men influenced each other through regular conversation, years of friendship and a similar theological disposition. Certainly Erskine's 1831 book, *The Brazen Serpent*, bears important similarities to Campbell's views on the atonement in his 1856 book, *The Nature of the Atonement*, but these similarities give evidence to the commonality in perspective both men shared. Campbell himself confirms this theory in a letter to his friend Robert Story, "That historical independence which we mark when two minds, working apart and without any interchange of thought, arrive at the same conclusions, is always an interesting and striking fact when it occurs; and it did occur as to Scott and myself; and also as to Mr. Erskine and me." Cf. R.H. Story, *Memoir of the*

Life of the Reverend Robert Story (London: Macmillan, 1862), p. 152.

54. *Memorials*, Vol. 1, p. 272.

55. For example, Campbell thought Erskine had an inadequate doctrine of the Holy Spirit in his last published book, *The Spiritual Order*. Cf. *Memorials*, Vol. 2, p. 345.

56. Thomas Chalmers (d. 1847), one of Scotland's most influential and orthodox churchman of this time, led the Free Church secession in 1843, called the Disruption. Chalmers was a close friend of both Irving and Campbell, although he was very different in spiritual temperament from them. It is curious that Chalmers, who could have exercised considerable influence, was absent and silent on the deposition proceedings against both Irving and Campbell. cf. Tuttle, *So Rich a Soil*, p. 61.

57. One commentator on Irving said that the appearance of pentecostal gifts in the London church was "greatly to the disturbance of staid old-fashioned people there." *The Religious Controversies of Scotland* by Henry F. Henderson (Edinburgh: T & T Clark, 1905), p. 119.

58. Henry F. Henderson, *The Religious Controversies of Scotland* (Edinburgh: T & T Clark, 1905), p. 121.

59. Edward Irving, *The Human Nature of Christ*, p. 91. (check this)

60. *Memorials*, Vol. 1, p. 54. Although Campbell clearly valued his friendship with Irving and mourned his death with great depth of feeling, some of Campbell's interpreters feel the association was not beneficial to Campbell's reputation. One Campbell interpreter regretted Campbell's connection with Edward Irving at all. He said that the name of Irving caused "some of the worst aspersions cast on Campbell and his work." Cf. Bewkes, *Legacy of a Christian Mind*, p. 2.

61. Otto Pfleiderer, in his history of doctrine, claims that John McLeod Campbell had no dependence on German theology at all, that his theology arose independently of Continental influence. Cf. *The Development of Theology in Germany Since Kant and its Progress in Great Britain Since 1825*, 3rd ed., trans. J. Frederick Smith (London: Swan Sonnenschein & Co., Ltd., 1909), p. 382.

62. *Memorials*, Vol. 2, p. 201.

63. *Memorials*, Vol. 2, p. 202. Campbell's own terse and abbreviated remarks are: "As to religion, he never lost altogether what his early Moravian training had quickened in him, and its power seemed greatest towards the close; but his faith rather acknowledged God as the source of all that others were to him - of his own and their capacities of love - than as hearing and responding to the love which says, 'My son, give Me thine heart.' He thought he was able to co-ordinate his religion and his philosphy, as Jacobi found himself able to do; but I could not but fear that his philosphical difficulties as to the personality of God affected his heart's Godward movements."

64. There is no evidence of acquaintance between Campbell and Bushnell other that the latter's acknowledgement of his "profound respect" for Campbell's work in the preface of his *Forgiveness and Law* (New York: Armstrong, 1874). Bushnell's other important book on the atonement is *The Vicarious Sacrifice: Grounded in Principles Interpreted by Human Analogies* (New York: Charles Scribner's, 1903).

65. These characteristics are clearly evident in *The Nature of the Atonement*, where Campbell explicitly states them in every context. Cf. also Brian Gerrish, *Tradition and the Modern World; Reformed Theology in the Nineteenth Century*, p. 95.

66. *Memorials*, Vol. 2, p. 341, 342.

67. *Memorials*, Vol. 2, p. 334.

68. *Memorials*, Vol. 2, p. 335.

69. *Memorials*, Vol. 1, p. 339.

CHAPTER TWO

THE STRUCTURE OF CAMPBELL'S
ATONEMENT THEOLOGY

Motivation of Campbell's Theology

Campbell's atonement theory was motivated by the experiences of his pastoral ministry with a congregation who found it difficult to have a confident assurance of their faith. Convinced that this restlessness and fear was an unhappy effect of a theology gone wrong, Campbell tried in his preaching to summon them away from their concern about their election and look instead to the forgiveness and love of God's grace. He says, for instance in an 1828 letter to his father, "It has become the epidemic disease of the present age that men should find peace in the combination of an orthodox creed with much religious bustle; but *heart religion* has been long at a low ebb."[1] A 1832 letter to his sister echoes a similar thought, "I feel that with many the simplicity of the truth gives an impression of superficiality; while I feel that, in point of fact, that searching of heart is superficial which admits of rest in anything else than a simple faith in God."[2]

One primary basic, underlying concern can be discerned in Campbell's entire pastoral ministry as well as his work on the atonement, namely, his desire to highlight and make primary the love of God. In his memoirs written near the end of his life, Campbell remembers how he tried in his sermons, "to fix their attention on the love of God revealed in Christ, and to get them into the mental attitude of looking at God to learn His feelings toward them, not at themselves to consider their feelings toward Him."[3] The first word of the Christian pastor, or the first principle of a stated atonement theory, must be the forgiving love of God. Not the demands of the law, not the guilt of the sinner, not the offended honor of God. The only "prerequisite" of the gospel Campbell is willing to concede is full confidence in God's love. "The first demand which the gospel makes upon us in relation to the atonement is, that we believe that **there is forgiveness in God**."[4] There is a hint of Campbell's exasperation with his fearful people when he remarks, "For it ought not to be difficult to believe that, though we have sinned against God, God still regards us with a love which has survived our sins."[5]

The foundational presupposition of Campbell's atonement theory, therefore, is his doctrine of God.[6] His congregation tended to think of God as vengeful, demanding the punishment of Jesus Christ for the sin which dishonors God's name. On this view, Christ's sufferings were punishment that God inflicted. Campbell believed that Christ's sufferings had an entirely different function. That is, Christ saw and felt the full horror and scandal of sin by seeing sin and sinner with God's eyes and experiencing the feelings of God's own heart with regard to sin.[7] This difficult question of the nature of Christ's sufferings will be examined at several points below; the aim here is to make clear Campbell's foundational principle which infuses his entire atonement theology, namely, that God is a God of love, not of vengeance or punishment or retribution. Campbell, of course, was exploring the old and difficult problem of the relation between the love and justice of God. His solution emphatically denied that there is a conflict between God's love and justice. Campbell was determined to highlight the **love** of God.

A second basic motivation which arises from Campbell's primary concern to emphasize the love of God has to do with the relationship between the Incarnation and the atonement. It was Campbell's belief that the atonement should be viewed always as a natural continuation of the Incarnation. Campbell wished to distance himself from traditional Calvinism's legal conceptuality in which Christ's benefits won by the atonement are rather externally and arbitrarily imputed to the human believer. Rather, he insisted on a participation of the human believer in the life of Christ as a natural outcome of the atonement, which, in turn, was a natural outcome of the Incarnation. Campbell explains,

... the connection between the atonement and our participation in the life of Christ is not arbitrary, but natural: and thus the incarnation, the atonement, and man's participation in the divine nature offer to our faith one purpose of divine love, reaching its fulfillment by a path which is determined by what God is and what He wills that man should be.[8]

The word "natural" appears frequently in Campbell's *The Nature of the Atonement*, not only in his brief methodological comments, but throughout the development of the book. By this word, Campbell means to express the idea that the meaning of the atonement is to be interpreted from the facts of Christ's life on earth, not from any external requirements such as the justice of God or the demands of the law. All the events in the life and death of Christ are "self-evident" for Campbell; they reveal their meaning without the need for an arbitrary, external frame of reference.

Thus, as the above quote indicates, the atonement itself is a natural development of the Incarnation. Campbell sees it as self-evident that, given the Incarnation, the atonement followed, in the form that it did occur. Furthermore, each of the elements of the atonement such as the suffering of Christ, the death of Christ and the believer's participation in the life of Christ, all follow as clear developments of the life of Christ. Campbell's concern is to avoid imposing a framework of interpretation on the events of Christ's life so as to construct a theory of the atonement. Rather, he wishes to let the facts speak for themselves, facts which he believes yield an understanding of the atonement.

This notion of the "natural" development of the atonement presents a challenge for the interpreter of Campbell. Campbell himself did not explain the content of the idea; he seems to consider it self-explanatory. He did not demonstrate how his theory is a natural interpretation in contrast to others which he sees as arbitrary. He just states that his atonement theology is "natural." It remains a bare assertion. This study of Campbell's atonement account will attempt to interpret Campbell's use of the word "natural" when it arises in an important context. As a general rule, "natural" means an interpretation which starts from the facts of Christ's life on earth as recorded in the Scriptures rather than an interpretation which starts from an external point of inquiry such as the necessity, or possibility of the atonement.

Methodology

John McLeod Campbell is explicit in the opening pages of *The Nature of the Atonement* about his methodology. He says, "I have in this volume approached the subject of the atonement from the side of faith; in some sense writing for those who believe that they may believe."[9] Thus, Campbell joins in the line of theologians who attempt to articulate the faith for believers. **Fides quaerens intellectum** would be as apt a methodological summary for Campbell as it was for Augustine, Anselm and Karl Barth. For Campbell, this theological approach found its source in two basic concerns. One has already been noted above - the experience of his parish ministry. Because Campbell was dismayed at the anxious, fearful state of his congregation's spiritual health, he was determined to see the atonement from the point of faith in a loving, forgiving God.

The other source for Campbell's methodological principle, that is, to approach atonement from the perspective of faith in a loving God, was prompted by his analysis of the cultural and intellectual climate of the day. In the introduction to *The Nature of the Atonement*, Campbell identifies two contextual influences which, in his view, hindered or inhibited belief in the atonement. The first was the familiar Enlightenment belief in human progress and human reason, making any notion of atonement unnecessary or superfluous.[10] The second influence was a cluster of ideas, including universal causes, natural law, and the mechanistic, determined nature of the world. Campbell concluded that these ideas made belief in a loving, personal, active God quaint or incongruous.[11]

The brief methodological remarks in the introduction to *The Nature of the Atonement* are far short of a fully explicit methodology. They do indicate, however, that Campbell was aware of and sensitive to the cultural conditions of his own time but yet believed that the Christian gospel can and should have a word even in times of human self-sufficiency and scientific self-confidence. He challenged the intellectual community, saying that it is "altogether reasonable to ask from scientific men that they should first deal with the claim which the kingdom of God makes on their faith. . ."[12] Thus, Campbell's methodological preference for reflection based on faith emerged both from the experiences of his pastoral ministry as well as from reflection on the intellectual and cultural milieu of the mid-nineteenth century.

For Campbell, beginning from faith means beginning with a proper humility to remain open and obedient to the "light of the Truth," or the divine light.[13] That is, the "light of love. . . is so full of self-evidencing light" that it authenticates the claims of faith.[14] The image of "light" is an important one for Campbell throughout his atonement theology. It is an image intended to convey what is self-evident or self-authenticating about the atonement. Here, it appears as part of his defense for the priority and sufficiency of the claims of faith. He says, "The attitude of the spirit towards God in faith is so truly its right and most excellent attitude. . . that the demand for it is felt to be made in pure light, and he who makes it is felt to be holding forth the word of life."[15] Campbell is claiming that faith is sure and confident because the God that faith professes is active and responsive and initiating in the faith process. Faith is sure because God confirms it. Faith is sure because it is **God** that faith confesses, not some object but the living, loving, active God.

In *The Nature of the Atonement*, Campbell does not defend and explicate his methodological principle in detail. But a couple of years after the publication of Campbell's book, several events took place in England that prompted Campbell's further reflections on the broader issues of revelation, authority, inspiration, and relative criteria for religious claims. Those events were the 1858 Bampton lectures by the Oxford scholar H.L. Mansel, *The Limits of Religious Thought Examined*, and the 1860 appearance of the controversial volume, *Essays and Reviews*.

Mansel's famous lectures aroused heated debate in England and Scotland. The lectures had to do with the problem of religious knowledge. His intent was to defend true religious knowledge by debunking the claims of rationalism, dogmatism, and moralism and by promoting revelation.[16] Reason is not the judge of revelation; rather, revelation is superior to reason and needs no authorization from rational human capacity.[17]

Mansel's argument took on a particularly conservative direction when he declared that God's revelation is the Bible and the Bible must be accepted in whole as revelation by the evidences of prophecy and miracles. To criticize the voice of the Bible is to discredit the entire Christian religion. One must accept all or nothing.[18] The Bampton lectures provoked vigorous response from a number of prominent British thinkers, including F.J.A. Hort and F.D. Maurice. These thinkers strongly objected to what they perceived to be a narrow, propositional, and biblicistic view of revelation in Mansel's account.[19]

Two years later, in 1860, the volume *Essays and Reviews* was published and it too produced a storm of controversy.[20] *Essays and Reviews* was a collection of seven essays on the subject of biblical interpretation which set a new course for biblical scholarship in England. It took a liberal stance with respect to the use of historical criticism and attempted to break free from the constraints of orthodoxy in the Church of England.

Campbell's reaction to both Mansell and *Essays and Reviews* was mixed. He believed both volumes, as different as they are, approached important truths but also that both volumes were in error. In accord with Mansel, Campbell held a strong view of the trustworthiness of Scripture. In contrast to Mansel and in accord with the *Essays and Reviews'* authors, he welcomed the tools of historical criticism in biblical scholarship. In contrast to the authors of *Essays and Reviews*, he wished to maintain a vital sense of inspiration. Campbell felt that this volume erred in viewing the Scriptures with critical assumptions already in place, rather than with an attitude of trust and expectation. He said in a letter to his son, "What I am jealous of is, not the conclusions of a fair criticism, but certain assumptions as to what is antecedently believable and unbelievable, which hinder fair criticism . . ."[21] The correct approach to the

Scriptures, Campbell believed, depends "on the measure of prepared-ness to welcome and respond to what God is teaching."[22]

Campbell responded further to both these publications in his 1862 book, *Thoughts on Revelation with Special Reference to the Present Time*. Campbell believed both Mansel and the *Essays and Reviews'* authors missed the internal, self-evident, inherent authority of the Bible. One does not need external evidence of the truth of the Christian experience and the authority of the Bible.[23] Rather, a "true Revelation of God must be its own witness."[24] He explains,

> If when I am asked, "How do you know that the Bible is a divine Revelation?" I thus answer, "Because it reveals God to me," am I to be met by the further question, "How do you know that it is God that it reveals?" To such a question, the most solemn that can be addressed to a man, the answer is, that God is known as God by the light of what He is. If the Bible places me in that light, it makes me to know God and to know that I know God with a pure and simple and ultimate certainty, to which no certainty in any lower region can be compared.[25]

Thus, for Campbell, the authority of the Scriptures comes from an experience of having been met by God, of having known God as the light of certainty and truth. There is no need for irrefutable scientific evidence or authoritarian ecclesial decrees. Instead, the authority of the Scriptures comes from the believer's experience of the revelation of God, that is, God's gift of Godself. "So God gives Himself to us in giving us the capacity of knowing and enjoying what He is."[26]

As a result of God giving us this capacity to recognize Godself, revelation in general and the Bible in particular are validated by the experience of the believer as encountered by God. Campbell was fully aware of the philosophical and epistemological challenges to such a view. But he was convinced that the religious experience as relation to God was ultimately valid.[27] Reason and judgement can be, and are, part of the religious experience; Campbell does not hold to a one dimensional definition of experience-as-feeling. But reason and judgement cannot invalidate or rule out the voice of experience because God is the one who is the source of that experience.

Campbell's fundamental presupposition of faith as an experience of encounter with God was not fully articulated until his book *Thoughts on Revelation* in 1862. But the basic contours of his theory of revelation are apparent in *The Nature of the Atonement* and had extensive influence for his atonement theology. His conviction that faith is the believer's irrefutable experience with a loving, forgiving God supplied Campbell with his approach to the doctrine of the atonement. It was inconceivable to Campbell that God might need to be avenged or God's wrath appeased. It was unthinkable that God might require a cosmic audit and balance the books by means of Christ's death. It was completely contrary to the nature of a loving God to exact a penalty from Christ equivalent to the offense of human sin. Rather, God is the Loving Father; it is from this foundation that all subsequent considerations on the atonement must be made. For Campbell, this is axiomatic. "But if God provides the atonement, then forgiveness must precede atonement; and the atonement must be the form of the manifestation of the forgiving love of God, not its cause."[28]

Campbell's Critique of Calvinism

The organization of *The Nature of the Atonement* is such that Campbell's own theory is not constructively explicated until the sixth and seventh chapters. In chapters one to five, Campbell occupies himself with several other tasks. First, he analyzes Luther's commentary on Galatians, where he finds in Luther support for an important theme in his own atonement theory, namely, the full identification of Christ with the believer. So much does Christ identify with the believer, that Christ's bearing our sins "was a deep and painful reality in his own mind."[29] This theme of Christ's identification with us and the way in which Christ bore our sin is one of the most pivotal and controversial of Campbell's themes. It will be considered at some length in chapter four below in a discussion of key difficulties in Campbell's atonement theology.[30]

Another focus of Campbell's attention in the early chapters of his book was a critical survey of the Calvinism of the 17th and 18th centuries as well as representative Calvinist theologians of his own day. That Campbell did not go back to study Calvin himself is a highly significant omission. The question arises whether he was operating with the assumption that Calvin's atonement theology is identical with Calvinism and so passed over it for reasons of economy or if he avoided Calvin for some other reason. Because Campbell was motivated by the desire to redirect people's attention **away** from the Calvinism of Scotland to a new conception of the atonement, it is perhaps not surprising that he did not examine Calvin's teachings themselves but focused instead on the Calvinism of his day he wished to refute. The irony of this feature of Campbell's book is that his proposed atonement theology bears striking and important similarities to Calvin's theology and thus, perhaps unwittingly, Campbell re-established in his book a line of continuity from Calvin that had been lost in the centuries of Calvinism after Calvin.[31]

The Calvinism that Campbell examines in chapters three, four and five are of "two very distinctly marked forms," as Campbell put it.[32] Chapter three looks at the Calvinism of John Owen (1616-1683) and Jonathan Edwards (1703-1755). These Calvinists represent classic Calvinism's emphasis on penal substitutionary atonement.[33] Chapter four looks at "modified Calvinism," represented by Campbell's older-contemporaries, John Pye Smith (1774-1851), George Payne (1781-1858), and Thomas W. Jenkyn (c. 1846), all of England, and Ralph Wardlaw (1779-1853), of Scotland. These later Calvinists represent, for Campbell, federal Calvinism with its atonement theory based on rectoral justice. Both systems he renounces as inadequate to portray the love of God and incapable of eliciting from human believers full awareness of their status as adopted sons and daughters. A closer look at Campbell's critique of both sets of Calvinists will help make Campbell's own theory more distinctive and intelligible.

Campbell's primary objection to the Calvinism of Owen and Edwards is one of method; he asserts that both Owen and Edwards reflected on the work of Christ in light of what they held as the foundational divine attributes of righteousness and holiness.

Campbell, as noted above, believes that all theological reflection, including reflection on Christ's work, must be done in the light of Christ's life, which clearly exhibits the love of God. He responds to the criticism that such a theological principle as the love of God will result in "a meagre and sentimental piety."[34] While he acknowledges the importance of keeping in view the idea of God as Judge, he nonetheless insists that the idea of God as Father must be the root idea of which the idea of God as Judge is secondary and derivative.

Thus, Campbell disputes the Calvinism of Owen and Edwards from the point of fundamental presuppositions and method. He calls the methodological mistake of the Calvinists an "axiomatic defect," one that negatively influences the whole system of this type of Calvinism.[35] It is a fundamental methodological issue characteristic of Protestant Scholasticism in general.[36]

A more specific objection of Campbell to the Calvinism of Owen and Edwards regards their doctrine of limited atonement. Campbell's reason is characteristic, "I am unable to see any way out here, or any escape from the conclusion, that the doctrine of an atonement for the elect only, destroys the claim of the work of Christ to be what fully reveals and illustrates **the great foundation of all religion, that God is love.**"[37] By now, it is not hard to see how consistently Campbell applies his basic theological principle of the love of God. Campbell is impressive in this respect, unrelenting in his determination to perceive everything from this perspective.

Chapter four of Campbell's book continues the critique of Calvinism, this time through the writings of his near contemporaries of England and Scotland. The Calvinism of this time was characterized by a shift in the conception of the demands of justice in the atonement from that of individual or distributive justice to rectoral justice. That is, on this view, instead of God demanding the punishment of Christ to be equivalent to the sum total of the punishment due to each human sinner, God demanded a punishment for Christ that substituted for deserved human punishment one appropriate to the good order of God's moral government. The Rectoral theory is considered a variant of the theory of penal substitution, although some of its key features are very different.

Campbell does admit that the modifications of these later Calvinists offer some improvements from the Calvinism of Owen and Edwards. Limited atonement seems to be discarded by the writers under observation; rectoral justice demands appear less morally repulsive than penal demands; the doctrine of the double decree has been eliminated. There is something, then, for which Campbell can be appreciative.[38] But he is not convinced that theories relying on rectoral justice conceptions characteristic of these later Calvinists are much better in the final analysis. Campbell notes that the function of Christ's sufferings remains much the same, that is, Christ's sufferings were the direct afflictions of the wrath of the Father against Christ.[39] Furthermore, the schemes remain mainly legal, not relational. This is considered by Campbell to be a fundamental problem in traditional Calvinist accounts of the atonement. For a legal conceptuality misconstrues the ultimate purpose of the atonement. The purpose of the atonement is not imputation of righteousness, what Campbell calls a "legal fiction," but rather a "condition of reconciled children trusting in the Father's heart and reposing on His love. . ."[40] That is, a relationship of filial trust is the ultimate purpose of the atonement.

Campbell thinks that the images, concepts, or metaphors of a range of atonement schemes must not necessarily be discarded. But they must fit in under the umbrella concept of the parental love of God. He asks rhetorically, "For do we not feel that, if the Eternal Father is satisfied, then must the Judge of all the earth be satisfied - that the provision which secures the fulfillment of the longings of the Father's heart, must secure the highest ends of rectoral government?"[41]

Before Campbell proposes a positive statement of his own atonement theory, he offers, in a fifth chapter in his book, a few more assessments of the systems of Calvinism he had critiqued. This is an important chapter, for it introduces a central concept in Campbell's atonement theology. That concept has to do with the function and nature of Christ's sufferings, a topic which is crucial to Campbell's argument. It will be recalled that Campbell objects to the penal and rectoral forms of atonement which construe Christ's sufferings as "commensurate with the eternal sufferings which were the doom of sin," a concept he finds morally repulsive.[42] Campbell resists the notion that Christ's sufferings were atoning or redemptive **as such**. He cannot see that there is any redemptive content in the doctrine that Christ's sufferings were punishment and in that punishment, somehow, we are saved.

Rather, Campbell insists that the sufferings of Christ were redemptive because of their connection to who Christ is and his relation to the Father and to humanity. How does this influence an understanding of Christ's sufferings? Instead of the sufferings being redemptive because they were punishment, Christ's sufferings should be seen as the form that the holiness and love of God takes in the glaring reality of sin. Campbell lays the options out like this: ". . . was it the pain as pain, as a penal infliction, or was it the pain as a condition and form of holiness and love under the pressure of our sin and its consequent misery, that is presented to our faith as the essence of the sacrifice and its atoning virtue?"[43] Clearly, Campbell chose the latter; Christ's sufferings were an expression of his love for the Father and his love for humanity and his complete solidarity with both.

Because Christ was fully divine, he suffered in the full realization of the horror of sin in the sight of God. Because Christ was fully human, he suffered by taking upon himself all the limitations of the human condition. But it is important to realize that these sufferings, although real in themselves, were not punishment. They were the form of divine love and the form of human confession. Campbell says, "Thus related to us, while by love identified with us, the Son of God necessarily came under all our burdens, and especially our great burden - sin."[44]

The theory of the function and nature of Christ's sufferings is an innovative feature of Campbell's atonement theology, one that he takes care to develop and defend. It is an issue central to Campbell's whole argument because his view of Christ's sufferings as a form of holiness in the face of the reality of sin challenges and refutes the theory of both the penal substitutionary and the rectoral forms of atonement theology prominent in Scotland at that time.

Campbell's Atonement Theology

The atonement theology of John McLeod Campbell is impressive on several counts. It is impressive in its consistency in exhibiting the basic presuppositions and principles described above. It is also impressive in its balance; the theory does not fall into an easy subjectivism which is concerned only with the experience of the human person nor does it take a stance of over-speculative certainty with respect to the inner, divine logic of the objective side of the atonement.[45] Campbell's own definition of the atonement demonstrates this scope and balance: ". . . the atonement is to be regarded as that by which God has bridged over the gulf which separated between what sin had made us, and what it was the desire of the divine love that we should become."[46]

The balanced nature of Campbell's atonement theology is further demonstrated by the structure of chapters six and seven in *The Nature of the Atonement*. Campbell organizes his discussion by proposing a pair of words, "retrospective" and "prospective," each of which will be examined from two directions, God-ward and humanity-ward. This pair of words, "retrospective" and "prospective," designates Campbell's central conviction that the atonement not only dealt with our sins and their offense to God but also guarantees our adoption as children of God and heirs to eternal life. The retrospective and prospective aspects of Campbell's atonement theology are captured in the subtitle of his book: *The Nature of the Atonement and its Relation to Remission of Sins and Eternal Life*. Remission of sins is the retrospective aspect; eternal life is the prospective aspect. Thus, these two words designate an expansive scope and an inclusive temporal framework, as will be illustrated below.

From this pattern of organization, Campbell has four features of his atonement theory to ponder. The first two belong to the retrospective aspect. They are Christ dealing with humanity on the part of God and Christ dealing with God on behalf of humanity. In other words, Christ, in the work of the atonement, acts as a mediator between God and humanity by performing specific acts appropriate for God or of God as well as for humanity or of humanity, in both life and death, to accomplish the goal of reconciliation.

The prospective aspects of the atonement as well specify the two directions of Christ in the work of the atonement: toward God and toward humanity. Christ witnesses for the Father to humanity and Christ intercedes with the Father on behalf of humanity. In other words, Christ continues to act as a mediator in order to accomplish further salvific benefits beyond that of dealing with the remission of sin. Prospectively, Christ assures our status of adopted children and guarantees our hope of eternal life.

The rest of this chapter will explore each of these elements in turn and will then address itself to the question of the overall coherence and completeness of Campbell's atonement theory. Campbell himself emphasizes that examining the atonement from the perspective of four aspects should not obscure the unity and simplicity of the life of Christ. Jesus Christ did not accomplish his salvific work, so to speak, from a job description with several objectives. Rather, he came in one life of love to God and love to humanity. Campbell calls the life and work of Christ a "pervading unity" which "will not be veiled by this orderly consideration of the different aspects of the works of Christ. . ."[47]

Retrospective Aspect of the Atonement. As summarized above, the atonement is **retrospective** both God-ward and humanity-ward. That is, Christ in the atonement mediates with people on behalf of God and with God on behalf of people. The first feature, Christ dealing with humanity on the part of God, focuses on how Christ witnessed to the love of God in his life on earth and in his relationships with people. Specifically, the perfection of Christ's humanity, which included both his love of the Father and his love of his fellow human beings, attested the trustworthiness of the Father's heart of love. Christ dealt with humanity on the part of God by perfectly demonstrating in his life and death the love of God.

But even though Christ was "a living epistle of the grace of God," he was repaid with hostility and anger. Because of rejection by those around him, Christ suffered. Yet Christ's bond of love and trust in the Father remained. In spite of his suffering, he still experienced a "joy deeper than the sorrow," a joy and a peace that even Christ's sufferings could not cancel.[48]

What was the purpose of Christ's sufferings? Campbell's answer, in an important sense, confirms that of the Calvinist tradition - as a sacrifice for sin. But, in contrast to the tradition, Christ's sufferings were not penal in character. Rather they were "endured in sympathy with God and in the strength of the faith of the divine acceptance of that sympathy."[49] In other words, the sufferings were a **perfection** of Christ's witness of his Father to humanity because the sufferings demonstrated Christ's zeal for God and Christ's complete sympathy for God's condemnation of sin. In this way they are a self-giving sacrifice for sin. They do not meet, in an external and arbitrary manner, some demand for divine justice but instead they are themselves the actual presentation of what our sins are to the Father's heart.

This is a critical concept for Campbell, one for which he has received both dismissive criticism and warm praise. It is important to understand the redemptive purpose and result of Christ's sufferings. Sufferings are not a punishment but are actually a revelation of the heart of God. Of Christ's afflictions Campbell says, ". . . the suffering is the suffering of divine love suffering from our sins according to its own nature. . ."[50] This clause reveals the crucial nature of Christ's sufferings for Campbell, that the sufferings are not penal in nature; they have a natural connection to the heart of the Father, and they are a true revelation of God. Because Christ is of one nature with the Father and because the Father experiences anguish over sin, so Christ experiences suffering. This is a "natural" connection for Campbell. Furthermore, the sufferings are themselves a witness to God's love. Put simply, the sufferings of Christ are what could only be expected when the love of God, perfectly revealed in Christ, comes into contact with human sin.[51]

The second feature of the retrospective aspect of the atonement has to do with Christ dealing with God on behalf of humanity. Here Campbell introduces the innovation in atonement theology for which he is most well known. The origin of this innovation Campbell traces to a treatise on the atonement by Jonathan Edwards. Edwards, in

that treatise, was reflecting on the principle that sin must be accounted for in the sight of God, "that sin must be punished with an infinite
punishment. . . unless there could be such a thing as a repentance,
humiliation and sorrow for this (sin) proportionate to the greatness
of the majesty despised. . .," that there must be, "either an equivalent
punishment or an equivalent sorrow and repentance."[52]   But then
Edwards dismissed the second of those options without further
deliberation, namely, that an equivalent sorrow and repentance could
be the satisfaction for sin.

It was this suggestion, so quickly discarded, that caught Campbell's attention. He felt that Edward's alternative to an equivalent
punishment was promising. Either of Edward's options could be seen
as "equally securing the vindication of the majesty and justice of God
in pardoning sin."[53]   The possibility of accounting for God's judgment on sin without the accompanying idea of punishment fit well
with Campbell's presupposition that the atonement must display the
love of God. Therefore, Campbell concluded that the way in which
Christ expiates humanity's guilt and propitiates God's wrath was by
making a perfect confession of humanity's sin.

In two frequently-quoted sentences, Campbell lays out his theory:
"That oneness of mind with the Father, which towards man took the
form of condemnation of sin, would in the Son's dealing with the
Father in relation to our sins, take the form of a perfect confession
of our sins. This confession, as to its own nature, must have been **a
perfect Amen in humanity to the judgment of God on the sins of
man."**[54]

Although the heart of Campbell's theory is contained in those two
highly condensed sentences, they are far from immediately clear and
lucid. Campbell's point here is that Christ offered a perfect response
to God's verdict on sin. The response was such that God's judgement
on sinners is averted because a perfect confession of human sin was
made in Christ. P.T. Forsyth extended this seminal concept of
Campbell, "As with one mouth, as if the whole race confessed
through Him, as with one soul, as though the whole race at last did
justice to God through His soul, He lifted up His face unto God and
said, 'Thou art holy in all Thy judgements. . .' "[55]

The nature of Christ as fully human and fully divine is important for Campbell's theory of Christ's perfect response to God. As fully human, Christ confesses human sin; as fully divine, Christ recognizes the weight and gravity and truth of God's verdict against human sin. Thus, it is only in the "divine humanity" of Christ that the Amen is possible; the Amen of Christ to the judgment of God of sin was a perfect response, one that "absorbed" God's judgment.[56]

Campbell explains why this confession of Christ in his "divine humanity" was efficacious: the repentance, the contrition, the sorrow were all done in "absolute perfection." Christ did for us what we could not do - he representatively repented for us in his "divine humanity" in a way that completely satisfied the wrath and justice of God.[57] Because Christ was acting for humanity in perfect "divine humanity," it was appropriate and possible for him to give an Amen to God's judgment on sin. Because Christ fully accepted and understood the gravity and destructive power of sin, he could fully repent for that sin, on behalf of all humanity.

In summary, the retrospective aspect of the atonement described above has as its primary purpose in Campbell's theology the remission of sins. Toward that end, the retrospective aspect contains two basic ideas. The first basic idea is Christ's dealing with humanity on the part of God. That is, Jesus perfectly loved his fellow human beings and submitted to the suffering which sin inevitably entails. Christ's sufferings demonstrate God's sorrow on account of the sin of humanity. They witness God's love to humanity. The key concept is the sufferings of Christ.

The second basic idea of the retrospective aspect is Christ's dealing with God on behalf of humanity. Jesus perfectly repented for our sins. In solidarity with all humanity, Jesus bore the full impact of divine judgment on sin by his perfect repentance. The key concept is the perfect repentance of Christ. By this repentance, in Christ, humanity receives God's judgement as right and holy, and by this perfect repentance, God is satisfied.

56

Prospective Aspect of the Atonement. The second main aspect of the atonement, on Campbell's scheme, is the prospective aspect. As in the retrospective aspect, the prospective aspect is organized in two "directions" or subheadings, the Godward direction and the direction toward humanity.

The prospective aspect has to do with the present and future results of the actions of Christ during his life and on the Cross, the positive blessings conferred by Christ's whole life and death. It is a mistake to regard this prospective aspect of the atonement as "subjective," in the sense that it is commonly used, namely, the effect of Christ's saving work on the believer. For Campbell, one cannot separate the objective and subjective so neatly. The two parts are mutually related and interdependent. In a letter to his sister, he reflects on this, ". . . in the light of the nature of the atonement the transition from objective to subjective religion, and back from subjective to objective, is necessary and constant."[58]

So, for Campbell, the prospective aspect of the atonement, although specifically having to do with eternal life, quite naturally pulls in the wide scope of the saving work of Christ. It includes both the continuing activity of Christ as well as the response of the believer. Campbell, in fact, explicitly says that the prospective aspect of the atonement implies both parts of the retrospective aspect of the atonement considered above. Christ's confession of our sins (retrospective) implies our participation in that confession (prospective). In addition, Christ witnessing for the Father exposed and judged the full darkness of our sin (retrospective) but also revealed the light of life desired by God for us (prospective).[59]

Campbell is interested, as always, in making the "practical ends of the atonement" a natural continuation and a connection with the "making of the atonement."[60] His concern is to make clear the connections between the various parts of the doctrine of the atonement. Furthermore, he is concerned to emphasize the natural, organic, purposive character of those connections. That is, the retrospective aspect, defined as "that by which God has bridged over the gulf which separated" God from humanity, cannot be considered apart from the prospective aspect, "what it was the desire of the divine love that we should become."[61] Campbell believes that this crucial connection has been missed or muted in traditional atonement accounts. He believes that, for instance, on the penal substitutionary view of the atonement, the punishment of Christ is considered separately from the imputation of righteousness on the elect and that the relation between those two aspects is not entirely clear or compelling. He is convinced that his own view is a significant improvement: ". . . the pardon of sin is seen in its true harmony with the glory of God, only when the work of Christ, through which we have 'the remission of sins that are past,' is contemplated in its **direct** relation to 'the gift of eternal life.' "[62]

Campbell believes that one must view the retrospective elements of the atonement from the position of the prospective, or, in other words, one must consider the remission of sins from the position of the hope of eternal life. Although he considers the retrospective aspect before the prospective aspect in his book, for Campbell, the experience of the believer is just the reverse; it is only from the perspective of the prospective aspect that the retrospective aspect has meaning.[63] Taking into account this experiential observation will, he thinks, keep "us from all this perplexity and confusing complication."[64]

The perplexity and confusing complication Campbell has in mind is the alternate view that the imputation theory suggests. He resists the traditional Calvinist idea of an imputation of Christ's righteousness to us, thinking it to be "a dishonour done to the divine righteousness."[65] Why is it a dishonor? Because for Campbell, a key criterion for an atonement theory is the natural connection between the work of the atonement and the effect or result of the atonement. Imputation is not natural, for Campbell; it is external.[66] Participation in the actual righteous life of Christ is natural; it is this concept then that Campbell chooses to explore. What this means is that the gift of perfect righteousness is ours by inclusion or participation in the perfect righteousness of Christ, not ours by imputation or some other external means of application to us. For Campbell, it is more natural, more fitting to start reflection on eternal life from the experience of having been graciously dealt with by God, rather than from the perspective of the requirements and conditions of eternal life.

With that general introduction into some of the contours and dynamics of the prospective aspect of the atonement, Campbell then addresses the specific content of the prospective aspect. The first part of the prospective aspect of the atonement is Christ witnessing for the Father to humanity; it is the direction toward humanity. Campbell is interested in exploring how Christ witnessed his perfect life of sonship to humanity, so that humanity can also share in that life of sonship.[67] How does Christ display his sonship and witness for the Father? For Campbell, this is accomplished by the whole life and death of Christ. Christ's perfect life of sonship not only revealed the Father's heart of love but also revealed the true nature of human persons. Campbell explains,

> I have said above that we are to understand that He who is the revealer of God to man is also the revealer of man to himself. Apart from Christ we know not our God, and apart from Christ, we know not ourselves: as, indeed, it is also true, that we are as slow to apprehend and to welcome the one revelation as the other - as slow to see man in Christ, as to see God in Christ.

He concludes by saying that we must "set ourselves to the study of the **twofold discovery of God and of man in Christ**, with the conviction that in it are hid for us all the treasures of wisdom and knowledge."[68] Only when the full "depth and reality of the bonds which connect the Saviour and the saved" are understood will a true understanding of the atonement be possible.[69]

Campbell excels in eloquence and passion in the section on the natural connection of Christ to the believer. His pastor's heart is clearly evident, for it is this aspect of the atonement that his congregation at Row was so slow to hear. The conviction that Christ perfectly shows us not only the Father's heart of love but also offers us participation in the life of sonship was what Campbell earnestly wanted his readers to share. He says, "Let us think of Christ as the Son who reveals the Father, that we may know the Father's heart against which we have sinned, that we may see how sin, in making us godless, have made us as orphans, and understand that the grace of God, which is at once the remission of past sin, and the gift of eternal life, restores to our orphan spirits their Father and to the Father of spirits His lost children."[70]

Campbell is so insistent in emphasizing the connection between Christ and the believer because he sees Christ as perfectly revealing the Father and so only in Christ and through the Spirit is the believer brought back to the loving heart of the Father. Multiple patterns of interrelatedness and bonds of love and trust are set up in Campbell's atonement theology, all of them with the ultimate goal of bringing the believer back to the heart of the Father. The Son reveals the mind of the Father; the Spirit guides the believer into the life that is Christ; the Father makes us heirs of God and joint heirs with Jesus Christ; the believer finds identity in the "unsearchable infinite riches" of adopted sonship.[71] In all of this, Christ is the center and the mediator of all these patterns and connections and bonds; it is in Christ, therefore, that the believer must find his or her identity.

The second part of the prospective aspect of the atonement is the God-ward direction in Christ's continual intercession to the Father for the sake of humanity. Campbell explicitly parallels this prospective intercession with the previously discussed retrospective confession of the sins of humanity; Christ's vicarious confession of our sins to the Father on the Cross has as its natural complement the continual intercession of Christ before the Father. Furthermore, just as Christ gave a perfect Amen to the judgment of God on the sins of humanity in his vicarious confession, so the believer can say Amen to that confession and enter into it. Campbell says that, "we get near to God just in the measure in which in the Spirit of Christ we thus lovingly adopt His confession of our sins. . ."[72]

In treating this element of the prospective aspect of the atonement, Campbell continues to be consistent and clear in connecting and relating it with the other elements: here, the confession of Christ (retrospective) and the intercession of Christ (prospective), "so harmonise, are so truly each the complement of the other, that we feel in passing from the one to the other our faith in the Father's acceptance of each confirmed by being in connexion with the other. . ."[73] The confession that Christ has offered to God on our behalf is to be taken up and reproduced in us. When, in faith, we accept God's judgment on sin, then we participate in the same mind of Christ which offered confession of sin and thus participate in the righteousness which pleases God.[74] Campbell says, "In the faith of God's acceptance of that confession on our behalf, we receive strength to say Amen to it - to join in it - and joining in it, we find it a living way to God. . . "[75]

It is Campbell's belief that this last element of the atonement, the Son dealing with the Father on behalf of humanity, most brilliantly displays the full light of the atonement. The whole loving desire of God to save is seen most clearly in this last element, the relationship between the Son on our behalf and the Father. The full acceptance of God for Christ's confession of our sins and the full acceptance of God for Christ's intercession on our behalf most convincingly demonstrates the "ultimate ground" of the atonement for Campbell, the love of God.[76]

In places, Campbell sounds like he is advocating a classic Moral Influence theory of the atonement in his consideration of Christ dealing with the Father on behalf of humanity. For instance, he says that, ". . . the superiority of a moral and spiritual atonement, consisting in the right response from humanity to the divine mind in relation to sin, becomes clear."[77] It is the infrequent statements such as this that some interpreters of Campbell have taken as warrant for a dismissal of him as a mere subjective theorist.[78] However, his intention is altogether different. He insists that shifting the focus from God as Judge to God as Father does not eliminate the need for an expiation of sin accomplished through the blood of Christ. Campbell uses surprisingly strong language with respect to the cleansing power of the blood of Christ, power the shed blood had to "consecrate a way for us" to the Father.[79]

What Campbell does not want is a vapid, naive, lenient view of the atonement. He asserts, in language almost echoing the penal language which he repudiates, "The Father's heart did demand the shedding of blood in order to the remission of sins because it demanded blood in which justice would be rendered to the fatherliness which had been sinned against. . . "[80] He repeats, and somewhat softens, that statement in the next paragraph, "We might, indeed, say that the Father's heart asked for an atonement for our sin, simply on the ground that it desired us back to itself. . ." In summary, the prospective aspect of the atonement, or the positive blessings which are conferred, contain two basic ideas for Campbell. The first basic idea is Christ's witnessing for the Father to humanity, witnessing God's desire that we be reconciled to God. In Christ we see the perfect human person and so receive direction and hope for inclusion as God's people. The key concept here is sonship, or inclusion and identification with Christ.

The second basic idea of the prospective aspect is Christ's dealing with the Father on behalf of humanity. In this, Jesus always continually offers himself to the Father in prayer and obedience. Christ intercedes for us and brings us into fellowship with God. The key concept in this idea is continual intercession of Christ before the Father.

Initial Evaluation of Campbell's Atonement Theology

An immediate and lasting impression one receives on a study of Campbell's atonement theology is that it is a very "big" concept of the atonement. The vision of Campbell's atonement theology takes in the whole sweep of God's divine plan to reach out and save lost humanity. It includes the eternal gracious intent of God, the life, death, and resurrection of Jesus Christ, the continuing activity of Christ on behalf of the believing community, and the active identification of the community with the living Christ. It embraces the traditional "objective" and "subjective" perspectives on Christ's work; in fact, as has been noted, Campbell quite explicitly states his intent not to choose one or the other approach, but to deal with both in their reciprocal relationship.[81] Perhaps because Campbell's atonement theology as explicated in *The Nature of the Atonement* has such scope and range, as well as numerous peculiarities of style and organization, it presents the reader with puzzles and problems which invite a wide variety of interpretations and a spectrum of conclusions about the place of Campbell in the history of atonement theology and the history of Reformed theology. The purpose of this interpretive study, as stated in the Introduction, is to make the case for the coherence of Campbell's atonement theology as well as Campbell's place in a line of continuity in the Reformed tradition, especially with reference to Calvin, with respect to basic foundational principles and key atonement concepts.

Besides the general observation that Campbell's atonement theology is expansive and encompassing, several additional characteristics can be noted. One of these characteristics is the method of organization Campbell employs in *The Nature of the Atonement*. In an attempt at clarity and coherence, Campbell organizes his theory by the four-fold classification described in this chapter. But such a classification holds the distinct danger of over-systematizing the atonement, a truth so rich and dense in the New Testament as well as throughout the history of Christian doctrine that a wide range of metaphors have been employed in an attempt to express it. Campbell knew this danger of a too zealous systematization of the central confession of the Christian faith. He specifically warned against an excessively-tidy arrangement of concepts in the doctrine of the atonement. But yet some interpreters of Campbell have forgotten his warnings against a fragmented, atomistic view of the atonement and have expounded his atonement theology in a way that leaves little room for the relational, organic, natural character of the atonement that Campbell continually emphasized. Campbell surely would be resistant to some of these schematic or diagrammatic interpretations of his theology.[82]

Another characteristic of Campbell's atonement theology is the influence and function of his foundational motivating principle on the whole of his atonement theology. One can best understand Campbell if one approaches Campbell's reflections on the atonement with Campbell's theological method or motivation in full view. That is, one's interpretive attempt on Campbell's views on the atonement must be made with full sympathy toward Campbell's own stated intent or goal in explicating the doctrine of the atonement so as not to distort or misconstrue him. That intent, continually stressed by

Campbell, was to highlight and make primary the love of God. Thus, Campbell's lengthy and somewhat complex atonement theory is not intended to be a *theory* at all; rather, it is intended to give an account of the experience of the Christian believer of having been dealt with graciously by God. Campbell's atonement theology is through and through an experiential theology. This, of course, is precisely the feature of his theology for which some interpreters of Campbell have swiftly dismissed him. This regrettable misunderstanding illustrates the failure to be alert to Campbell's theological motivations. As a result, some of Campbell's insights into the life and work of Christ are discarded. It can not fairly be said that Campbell is merely a theologian of inward experience or subjectivity. To characterize his theory as "a variation of the 'moral influence' theory" is to misunderstand thoroughly Campbell's atonement theology and his place in Reformed theology.[83]

A final characteristic of Campbell's atonement theology has been briefly mentioned in connection with the first characteristic identified above. That is, Campbell's atonement theology admits of much varied and, even, opposing interpretations. Key difficulties will be analyzed in greater detail below, but a few examples will illustrate the varied interpretations which have surrounded Campbell's atonement theology.

First, the concept of Christ's perfect repentance which is at the heart of Campbell's retrospective aspect of the atonement is not easy to grasp. Several issues are involved, all of which arise from an effort to understand just what it is that Campbell means in his explication of the "perfect confession" of Christ. This key idea in Campbell has been taken up appreciatively by some theologians, such as R.C. Moberly and P.T. Forsyth, but in their appropriation of the concept, it has mutated both in content and emphasis from what Campbell intended. Thus, it is crucial to consider carefully what Campbell's understanding of this aspect of his atonement theology might be. One initial inquiry is whether the term "vicarious repentance," coined by Campbell's interpreters, not Campbell himself, is an adequate or accurate designation of this concept.

64

A second difficulty, related to the first, has to do with the question of Christ's connection, or relationship, to the human believer. Since interpretation of Campbell on this issue is so varied, it may be fair to say that Campbell himself is not clear on this central Christological and soteriological question.[84]

A third difficulty is the crucial question of the nature of Christ's sufferings, one of the most widely recognized areas of difficulty in Campbell's atonement theology. Even the most ardent Campbell supporters acknowledge the multiple conceptual and scriptural problems which surround this question.

NOTES

1. *Memorials*, Vol. 1, p. 56.

2. *Memorials* Vol. 1, p. 102.

3. *Reminiscences*, p. 133.

4. John McLeod Campbell, *The Nature of the Atonement*, 6th ed. (London: James Clarke & Co., Ltd., 1959), p. 18, emphasis Campbell's. Subsequent references to this book will be indicated by the designation, *The Nature of the Atonement*, followed by the page.

5. *The Nature of the Atonement*, p. 18. Dozens of other examples could be given of this theme in Campbell's sermons, letters, and books. It was a theme he never tired of repeating in many contexts.

6. James B. Torrance, "The Contribution of McLeod Campbell to Scottish Theology," *Scottish Journal of Theology* 26 (1973), p. 303. This is the central thesis of Michael Jinkins' important book, *A Comparative Study in the Theology of Atonement in Jonathan Edwards and John McLeod Campbell* (San Francisco: Mellen Research University Press, 1993).

7. *The Nature of the Atonement*, p. 117.

8. *The Nature of the Atonement*, p. xxvii.

9. *The Nature of the Atonement*, p. xxiii.

10. *The Nature of the Atonement*, p. xxxi.

11. *The Nature of the Atonement*, p. xxxii.

12. *The Nature of the Atonement*, p. xxxiii.

13. *The Nature of the Atonement*, p. 392.

14. *The Nature of the Atonement*, p. 393.

15. *The Nature of the Atonement*, p. 393.

16. Reardon, *From Coleridge to Gore*, p. 227.

17. Reardon, *From Coleridge to Gore*, p. 236.

18. Henry L. Mansel, *The Limits of Religious Knowledge Examined* (Oxford: J. Wright, 1858), p. 155.

19. Cf. F.D. Maurice, *What is Revelation?* (London: Macmillan and Co., Ltd., 1859) and a collection of F.J.A. Hort's letters edited by his son, Arthur F. Hort, *The Life and Letters of F.J.A. Hort* (London: Macmillan and Co., Ltd., 1896), pp. 398 and 402.

20. *Essays and Reviews* (London: J.W. Parker, 1860).

21. *Memorials*, Vol. 2, p. 31.

22. *Memorials*, p. 29.

23. Bewkes, *Legacy of a Christian Mind*, p. 123.

24. John McLeod Campbell, *Thoughts on Revelation with Special Reference to the Present Time* (London: Macmillan and Co., 1869), p. 14.

25. Campbell, *Thoughts on Revelation*, p. 17.

26. Campbell, *Thoughts on Revelation*, p. 151.

27. Bewkes, *Legacy of a Christian Mind*, p. 140.

28. *The Nature of the Atonement*, p. 18.

66

29. *The Nature of the Atonement*, p. 48.

30. Cf. chapter four.

31. This line of continuity from Calvin to Campbell will be further explored and demonstrated below in chapter five.

32. *The Nature of the Atonement*, p. 50.

33. The oddity of Campbell grouping John Owen and Jonathan Edwards together will be explored below in chapter four. Here, these two theologians are considered exponents of "classic Calvinism," an admittedly loose term which intends to denote theologies with significant source dependence on Calvin but which themselves admit of greater specificity and precision. John Owen (17th c.) is usually considered a Puritan theologian; Jonathan Edwards (18th c.), due to the unique style, context, and content of his theology, is best categorized as a powerful individual voice in the Reformed tradition.

34. The phrase is that of Thomas Chalmers from his *Institutes*. Campbell quotes it in *The Nature of the Atonement*, p. 72.

35. *The Nature of the Atonement*, p. 54.

36. Brian G. Armstrong makes a similar point about methodology in his study, *Calvinism and the Amyraut Heresy* (Madison: The University of Wisconsin Press, 1969), where he says that scholasticism in Reformed theology significantly changed theological method. Basically, the change can be characterized as a switch from an analytic, inductive approach to a synthetic, deductive approach. In other words, theological reflection no longer began (as it did in Calvin, for the most part) from the experience of being dealt with graciously by God but rather from the perspective of the eternal purposes and will of God. The result of this can be seen dramatically in the highly speculative doctrine of divine decrees. Armstrong says, "Since the starting-point in theological formulation was the divine decrees, there was no alternative but to discuss the whole of soteriology in terms of divine predestination or reprobation" (p. 137). Campbell would agree with Armstrong's critique of scholasticism's shift of theological method.

37. *The Nature of the Atonement*, p. 65, emphasis mine.

38. *The Nature of the Atonement*, p. 78.

39. *The Nature of the Atonement*, p. 84.

40. *The Nature of the Atonement*, p. 102.

41. *The Nature of the Atonement*, p. 105.

42. *The Nature of the Atonement*, p. 114.

43. *The Nature of the Atonement*, p. 118.

44. *The Nature of the Atonement*, p. 127.

45. However, as was noted in note 5 in the Introduction, not every reader of Campbell agrees with the judgement that Campbell's theory is balanced. Some interpreters do, in fact, see his account as overly-subjective. I wish to demonstrate that this judgment is mistaken.

46. *The Nature of the Atonement*, p. 151. Note, at this initial stage of describing Campbell's account of the atonement, that God is the primary actor in the drama of reconciliation.

47. *The Nature of the Atonement*, p. 128.

48. Campbell says that Christ never lost that sense of joy and peace in the Father, not even in the cry of dereliction. See *The Nature of the Atonement*, pp. 275 ff.

49. *The Nature of the Atonement*, p. 133.

50. *The Nature of the Atonement*, p. 134.

51. A closer look at some of the unique difficulties of Campbell's concept of the sufferings of Christ will appear below in chapter four.

52. Jonathan Edwards, *Concerning the Necessity and Reasonableness of the Christian Doctrine of Satisfaction for Sin*, Ch. II, 1-3. Quoted by Campbell, p. 127. Note that this quote from Edwards exhibits a distinctive feature of the penal substitutionary view of the atonement, namely, that it was necessary for Christ's sufferings to be equivalent in amount to the total of human sin. This concept of equivalency is one of number or volume - a curious idea. Penal substitutionary atonement theorists implied that the total amount of human sin could be exactly quantified and, furthermore, that Christ's sufferings must be equal to that total amount of sin. In fact, Christ's sufferings had to just exceed the total amount, in order not only to satisfy

68

the demands of God's justice but also to give compensation for sin's insult of God's honor.

53. *The Nature of the Atonement*, p. 137.

54. *The Nature of the Atonement*, pp. 135,136. Emphasis Campbell's.

55. P.T. Forsyth, *The Work of Christ* (London, 1938), p. 150.

56. Both of these interesting terms are on pp. 136, 137. What Campbell might have meant by Christ's confession "absorbing" the wrath of God will be considered at further length below.

57. *The Nature of the Atonement*, p. 137. Campbell repeats this idea several times in this section in an effort to make his meaning clear. On p. 139, he says, "Without the assumption of an imputation of our guilt, and in perfect harmony with the unbroken consciousness of personal separation from our sins, the Son of God, bearing us and our sins on His heart before the Father, must needs respond to the Father's judgment on our sins, with that confession of their evil and of the righteousness of the wrath of God against them, and holy sorrow because of them, which were due, due in the truth of things, due on our behalf though we could not render it, due from Him as in our nature and our true brother; - what he must needs feel in Himself because of the holiness and love which were in Him - what He must needs utter to the Father in expiation of our sins when He would make intercession for us."

58. *Memorials*, Vol. 1, p. 276.

59. *The Nature of the Atonement*, p. 152.

60. *The Nature of the Atonement*, p. 153.

61. *The Nature of the Atonement*, p. 151.

62. *The Nature of the Atonement*, p. 154.

63. It is interesting to note here that Calvin may have had the same concern in mind in his organization of Book 3 of the *Institutes*. Calvin treated sanctification (or, regeneration) before he dealt with justification in Book 3, not getting to the topic of justification until chapter 11, after a full discussion of the shape of the sanctified Christian life in the first ten chapters. Although the reason why Calvin chose this ordering is never made explicit,

he hints at the reason in 3.11.1, "Of regeneration, indeed, the second of these gifts, I have said what seemed sufficient. The theme of justification was therefore more lightly touched upon because it was more to the point to understand first how little devoid of good works is the faith, through which alone we obtain free righteousness by the mercy of God . . . For unless you first of all grasp what your relationship to God is, and the nature of his judgment concerning you, you have neither a foundation on which to establish your salvation nor one on which to build piety toward God." Calvin placed a discussion of sanctification first, I am suggesting, in order to stress the believer's relationship to God under God's love and grace and then, and only then, a discussion of the judgment of God is appropriate.

This is precisely Campbell's concern. Although he follows the more common order, considering first matters having to do with the remission of sin and the judgment of God (retrospective) and then matters of sanctification and eternal life (prospective), he too is convinced that the retrospective can only be considered from the light of the prospective.

64. *The Nature of the Atonement*, p. 156. Campbell's methodology was briefly described at the beginning of this chapter.

65. *The Nature of the Atonement*, p. 155. See also p. 177.

66. That is, imputation seemed to Campbell an arbitrary, external act. But an important question about the function of imputation in the Reformers, especially Calvin, needs to be addressed. If imputation had become a merely legal, external divine act in the theologies of the Calvinists, did it have that function for Calvin? This question of continuity will be explored in a later chapter. It will be claimed that Calvin's doctrine of union with Christ is a significant response to Campbell's objections to external, legal imputation theories.

67. *The Nature of the Atonement*, p. 162.

68. *The Nature of the Atonement*, pp. 167,168. Emphasis mine.

69. *The Nature of the Atonement*, p. 161. The interesting issue of the nature of the connection between Christ and the believer, the nature of the identification of which Campbell speaks, will be considered below in chapters four and five.

70. *The Nature of the Atonement*, p. 171.

71. All of these inner-Trinitarian and Godhead - believer relationships are mentioned briefly by Campbell in *The Nature of the Atonement*, p. 169. Also in this context, Campbell does not miss an opportunity to emphasize that this identity between Christ and the believer and the life of sonship possible in Christ indicate that God is love.

72. *The Nature of the Atonement*, p. 182.

73. *The Nature of the Atonement*, p. 175.

74. "We are contented and thankful to begin our new life with partaking in the mind of Christ concerning our old life, and feel the confession of our sins to be the side on which the life of holiness is nearest to us, the form in which it naturally becomes ours, and in which it must first be tasted by us: for holiness, truth, righteousness, love must first dawn in us as confessions of sin." *The Nature of the Atonement*, p. 178.

75. *The Nature of the Atonement*, p. 182.

76. *The Nature of the Atonement*, p. 177.

77. *The Nature of the Atonement*, p. 184.

78. These interpreters are listed on p. 2, note 5.

79. *The Nature of the Atonement*, p. 184, ". . . the blood of Christ which hath consecrated such a way for us, must have power to cleanse our spirits from that spiritual pollution which defiles rebellious children. . ." Cf. also p.193, "But it is only when we understand that the shedding of the blood of Christ had direct reference to our relation to God as the Father of our spirits, and to the opening of a way in which we as rebellious children can return to the bosom of the Father's love, according to the truth of what the Father is, and what sonship is, that we see that 'having boldness to enter into the holiest by the blood of Jesus, by a new and living way which he hath consecrated for us through the veil, that is to say His flesh, and having an High Priest over the house of God,' is the same thing with the Son of God being to us a living way to the Father."

80. *The Nature of the Atonement*, p. 185.

81. *Memorials*, Vol. 1, p. 276.

82. For example, James B. Torrance, in, "The Contribution of McLeod Campbell to Scottish Theology," p. 311, proposes a diagram as a model to summarize Campbell's atonement theory. The model consists of parallel and vertical lines and arrows to indicate the interaction of retrospective and prospective in Campbell's theology. Of course, there is nothing inherently distorting about such a diagram whose intent is to clarify. It is fair to say, though, that Campbell's theory is more suited to relational metaphors than it is to rather static diagrams.

83. Cf. p. 2, note 5 for this comment of George Carey.

84. One of Campbell's early reviewers said Campbell apparently was advocating an "individualism" (or nominalism) with respect to the relationship between Christ and the believer. Campbell protested this analysis and claimed that he understood the distinction between realism and individualism and had succeeded in steering in the dark between the two philosophical options without depending on one or the other. Cf. *The Nature of the Atonement*, pp. 401, 402 for Campbell's response to this review which was written by James Martineau under the title "Mediatorial Religion" from *National Review*, April, 1856.

CHAPTER THREE

TYPOLOGIES OF ATONEMENT THEORIES

A frequent observation on Christian atonement theories notes their sheer variety and diversity. The diversity in theological reflection on the atonement finds its parallel, and its primary source, in the profusion of biblical images and metaphors which include images of sacrifice, ransom from bondage, victory over hostile powers, cleansing from impurity, reconciliation between those separated or alienated, and others. These biblical images of salvation are compounded and combined with the extravagant collection of titles or images of Christ in the New Testament. Often, the images are mixed or stirred together; Scripture does not seem particularly reserved about the multiplicity of images on the saving work of Jesus Christ.

The tradition of Christian reflection, on this biblical example, has produced an abundance of atonement ideas, as any standard account of the history of atonement theology records. Unlike the doctrine of the Trinity and Christology, no orthodox doctrine or statement of the atonement has been negotiated in an ecumenical council. Diversity, rather than uniformity, has characterized atonement theology; it continues to characterize current theological reflection on the atonement. Affirming this feature of the Christian theology, John Macquarrie says, "At the best, we can only hope to have a number of analogies and metaphors, correcting and supplementing each other but together conveying something of the mystery of the cross as it has been experienced in Christian faith."[1]

In order to bring some order to the potential confusion of the diversity of atonement theories and images, atonement theologians have formulated various atonement typologies, or schemes of classification. An atonement typology is a systematic theological effort to answer the question, put to any given atonement theory, "Just what kind of theory is this?" There are, not surprisingly, a number of typologies proposed in this attempt to organize the conceptual field.

This chapter will examine the purpose, function, and character of atonement typologies, or schemes of atonement organization and classification. It will also survey a number of atonement typologies in order to illustrate an important feature of atonement typologies. That feature is the criterion of organization which operates explicitly or implicitly in any given atonement typology. The survey of typologies will demonstrate how the criterion of organization, in fact, impacts and influences the status of the theories included in the typology.

The Function of Atonement Typologies

The sheer variety and diversity of atonement theories requires some sort of organization and classification. This task is attempted by an atonement typology. A typology can serve to highlight the important features, or an important feature, of atonement accounts. In addition, by giving the full range of metaphors and images with respect to Christ's life and work, an atonement typology can expand faith's field of vision and deepen faith's awareness of the breadth, depth, and height of the gracious love of God.[2]

However, whatever the conceptual or perspectival benefits that atonement typologies may yield, this particular task of theological organization has often been a test or measure for the perceived orthodoxy of the day. Theologians committed to a highly "objective" account of the atonement, for instance, reject those with strong "subjective" interests and, likewise, theologians devoted to "subjective" accounts expel from the discussion those who advocate "objective" claims.

Literature on the doctrine of the atonement teems with such stereotypic dismissals. For example, Hastings Rashdall's influential, but highly tendentious book, *The Idea of Atonement*, criticizes the objective theory of the atonement, which he virtually equates with the particular theory of penal substitution. Rashdall admits his strong predisposition against any substitutionary view, "I have assumed, without much formal argument, that it is a view which, when once its nature is thoroughly appreciated, neither reason nor conscience can accept."[3] Other accusations against objective theories include descriptions like "primitive," "unintelligible," "arbitrary," "illogical," or "immoral."[4] Quite simply, Rashdall utterly repudiates *any* attempt to propose an objective theory of the atonement.[5] But it is clear that Rashdall uses the term "objective" as a weapon, not as a descriptive tool of systematic theology.

Thus it can be seen that the terms "objective" and "subjective," or, the terms often assumed to be their synonyms, "penal substitution" and "moral influence" are frequently used for argumentative or polemical purposes. When these words are used not for description but rather for dismissal, their theological utility and function is seriously weakened.

A further example of the polemical use of the familiar pair of typological terms "objective" and "subjective" could well be the mixed reaction to Campbell's atonement theology. Although Campbell's atonement account was rejected in his own day because it was judged to be contrary to the Westminster Confession, since then it has been rejected - or, conversely, warmly embraced - not in reference to the Westminster Confession but rather in reference to whether it is perceived as an objective account or a subjective account. Thus, it can be seen in the specific case of John McLeod Campbell that how his atonement theology has been cataloged or classified has served either for its recommendation or its rejection. If Campbell's theory wears the label "subjective," it becomes suspect to some theologians; if it wears the label "objective," it becomes equally suspect to others. Thus, with John McLeod Campbell in particular, and any atonement theology in general, it is important to be able to answer the question, "What sort of theory is this?" in ways that are clear and descriptive, not polemical and argumentative.

A Survey of Atonement Typologies

As noted above, one of the most common ways of approaching the variety of atonement themes in the Scripture and in the tradition is a two-fold arrangement of "objective" and "subjective." On this scheme, Anselm traditionally holds the distinctive place of the objective atonement theorist and Abelard takes the lead as the subjective atonement theorist. This scheme has in its favor simplicity. However, it also runs serious risks of reductionism and inaccuracy. As has been noted, the theory of John McLeod Campbell has been subject to reductionist and inaccurate handling at the hands of interpreters who have attempted to employ the objective-subjective typology. Thus, it is important to determine the uses as well as the restrictions of this familiar two-fold typology.[6]

Another familiar atonement typology can be seen in Gustaf Aulen's classic book, *Christus Victor*.[7] There, Aulen accounts for the long history of atonement reflection with a three-fold interpretive grid. According to Aulen, an atonement theory is either of the classic type, the subjective type, or the Latin type. This approach is, like the objective-subjective typology, simple and direct. But it too invites distortions and errors. George Rupp, commenting on atonement typologies, believes that Aulen succumbs to the risks of reductionism and imprecision. He demonstrates Aulen's historical inaccuracies, conflations, oversimplifications and misreadings in the three types. Because Aulen's purpose in *Christus Victor* is to reclaim the classic type, that is, the Christus Victor model, he especially misconstrues the subjective type and the Latin type.[8] Rupp's critical evaluation of Aulen's book is shared by others who see in Aulen's book a sort of rough-and-ready typology useful for a very broad perspective but one notably lacking in intellectual fairness and clarity.[9]

Other atonement typologies abound. B. B. Warfield, writing at the end of the last century, identified "five chief theories of the atonement."[10] What is interesting about Warfield's typology is the criterion he uses to arrange atonement accounts. He says, "Perhaps as good a method as any other is to arrange them according to the conception each entertains of the person or persons on whom the work of Christ terminates."[11] In other words, atonement accounts are grouped according to the idea of whom Christ's work effects, impacts, or otherwise changes.

First, there are those theories which see the work of Christ **affecting Satan**, represented mostly by early theologians such as Augustine and Gregory the Great. However, this theory still appears in medieval theology and in the Reformation.[12] Second, there are those theories which see the work of Christ **affecting humanity physically**. By that, Warfield means a theory which posits humanity's participation in the life of Christ to be the primary salvific fact. Mystical union and divinization are some of the images which belong to this category. Historical examples include the Pseudo-Dionysius and those influenced by him, Schleiermacher, the Mercersburg School, and F.D. Maurice.

The third theory identified by Warfield conceives of the work of Christ as **affecting humanity to ethical action**. Warfield has in mind here the so-called "moral influence theories." He believes these theories "transfer the atoning fact from the work of Christ to the response of the human soul to the influences or appeals proceeding from the work of Christ."[13] In other words, on Warfield's account of this theory, what saves humanity is not the work of Christ but rather the person's response to the work of Christ. Warfield identifies Ritschl, Herrmann, Bushnell, and the Social Gospel theologians as exponents of this view.[14]

A fourth type of theory identified by Warfield construe the work of Christ as **affecting humanity primarily and God secondarily**. As example, Warfield identifies Grotius' Rectoral theory. On Grotius' view, the work of Christ impacts humanity first in inducing people to repentance and faith which then enables God to forgive, all for the proper functioning of world order and harmony. Other proponents of this atonement theory type, named by Warfield, include the Arminians, the eighteenth century Edwardseans, and the Methodists.[15]

Warfield's fifth, and last, atonement type includes theories which conceive the work of Christ as **affecting God primarily and humanity secondarily**. This is the theory Warfield warmly recommends. Significantly, Warfield includes Campbell in this category, although he qualifies his endorsement with the warning that Campbell's theory is the category's "lowest form."[16] After pointing out the weaknesses of Campbell's account, Warfield, perhaps grudgingly, admits that "the theory rises immeasurably above the mass of those already enumerated, in looking upon Christ as really a Saviour, who performs a really saving work, terminating immediately on God."[17] The highest form of this category is the satisfaction theory, the one that Warfield insists is the "Biblical doctrine." He describes it as follows:

> According to it, our Lord's redeeming work is at its core a true and perfect sacrifice offered to God, of intrinsic value ample for the expiation of our guilt; and at the same time is a true and perfect righteousness offered to God in fulfillment of the demands of His law; both the one and the other being offered in behalf of His people, and, on being accepted by God, accruing to their benefit; so that by this satisfaction they are relieved at once from the curse of their guilt as breakers of the law, and from the burden of the law as a condition of life; and this by a work of such kind and performed in such a manner, as to carry home to the hearts of men a profound sense of the indefectible righteousness of God and to make to them a perfect revelation of His love; so that, by this one and indivisible work, both God is reconciled to us, and we, under the quickening influence of the Spirit bought for us by it, are reconciled to God, so making peace - external peace between an angry God and sinful men, and internal peace in the response of the human conscience to the restored smile of God.[18]

Warfield further advances this theory by noting that all the great creeds of the Church as well as "leading doctors of the churches for the last eight hundred years" have advocated the satisfaction theory. Examples of these leading doctors, according to Warfield, include Turretin and the Protestant Scholastics, John Owen, Abraham Kuyper, and Charles Hodge.

Several interesting aspects of Warfield's account of atonement types emerge. First of all, his clear preference for this theory is unmistakable, casting all others in an unfavorable light. Second, although he does not explicitly identify substituted punishment as the means of satisfaction, it is clear that penal substitution is the form of satisfaction that Warfield prefers. Evidence for this includes his reference to an angry God and to the curse of human guilt which Christ's sacrifice covers.

Third, his description of the satisfaction theory, quoted at length above, invariably pulls in central elements of other theories as well. This is seen most clearly by the phrase, "to carry home to the hearts of men," which sounds suspiciously like the moral influence theory of which he is so critical. In principle, Warfield sees the various atonement theories as distinct theological options. In effect, his treatment of the theory he prefers demonstrates that the theories are not so neatly divided and, in fact, overlap, merge, or intersect.

The fourth feature is the preferential treatment the "highest" theory receives in Warfield's description. Unlike his treatment of the others, Warfield does not point out any of the excruciating difficulties of the satisfaction theory. Fifth, and most important, Warfield's criterion for arranging his atonement typology significantly influences his evaluation of specific atonement theories. His criterion was how the work of Christ is understood to impact or effect God and/or humanity. This criterion is certainly a legitimate one; it is, after all, the work of Christ understood in some way or other that is the heart of the atonement. But because Warfield's preference, which goes unstated, is for one particular construal of the work of Christ, the others, which construe the work of Christ differently, are judged by him to be lacking in coherence or vitality. Before the task of classification has even begun, Warfield has pre-determined, in large measure, which theories will gain his approval and which will fall short.[19] Those theories which are precise on the effect of work of Christ are deemed "higher" than those which concentrate on other aspects of atonement theology.

By looking carefully at Warfield's typology, it is evident that how a given atonement theory is classified and evaluated depends heavily on interpretive presuppositions. These same features can be perceived in any atonement typology. Any typology can serve as a method of recommending one particular theory and thus suppress conceptual problems in that particular theory. Any typology can give the impression that the various atonement theories are more distinct than they actually are. Warfield's typology illustrates how an atonement typology can extend beyond the descriptive to the polemical.

Several recent atonement doctrine accounts are instructive for this survey of atonement typologies as well. In his important, though often puzzling book, *The Christian Understanding of Atonement*, F.W. Dillistone, organizes atonement motifs into "two basic shapes or patterns" which he then sub-divides into four "analogues" and four "parables."[20] These two basic shapes function as "an imaginative pattern of comparison which somehow links the record of the death and resurrection of Christ with the wider experiences of mankind."[21] In other words, an atonement theory links the past event with the present reality in an interpretive framework.

The first main interpretive framework to be used on atonement theories Dillistone calls "analogues"; they deal with patterns of **corporate** experience and transcend lines of religion and culture. Although Dillistone claims that the analogues are common patterns or motifs in any religious and cultural system, he wishes to interpret the atonement in terms of Christian revelation. On this pattern, Jesus, in his suffering and death, acts in some corporately or representatively significant way which provides regeneration for the whole world.[22]

The second main interpretive framework Dillistone calls "parables"; they deal with examples of **individual** achievement. On this pattern, Jesus acts as a dramatic victor who conquers forces of evil.[23]

Dillistone thus divides all atonement theories into two categories based on the criterion of their application either to a corporate context or an individual context. Dillistone's criterion conceals multiple philosophical and theological presuppositions. But those presuppositions can be detected in Dillistone's approach to the doctrine of the atonement. He begins with observations of human alienation in individual, corporate, and cosmic realms, a common feature of all humanity. He then moves to an equally common feature of all human experience, the longing for a restoration of harmony. The concept of atonement speaks to that human longing.[24] From there, Dillistone focuses specifically on the revelation of God reconciling the world through Christ. In other words, he moves from a general diagnosis of the human predicament to specific application of the Christian answer to that predicament. Consequently, his criterion arises from his observation of the extent and depth of human alienation - both corporate and individual. The theories which are divided into the two categories give alternative, although not necessarily opposing, accounts of how the work of Christ restores harmony and effects reconciliation.

Dillistone's typology of atonement theories is interesting. His analogues - those having to do with the corporate significance of Jesus Christ - include the images of sacrifice, tragedy, compassion, and integration. The parables - those having to do with the individual context - include the images of redemption, judgment, forgiveness, and reconciliation. Why it is that the first list of images have to do with corporate existence and the second list with individual existence is not defended or explained. Apparently, Dillistone sees this as self-evident.[25]

George Rupp, in *Christologies and Cultures, Toward a Typology of Religious Worldviews*, employs a philosophical criterion for constructing an atonement typology. He explicitly isolates the philosophical issues behind the range of atonement theories and is thus instructive to this survey. Convinced that the standard objective-subjective dichotomy oversimplifies and disguises essential philosophical distinctions, Rupp see various atonement theories corresponding to the questions clustered around two basic philosophical issues.[26] The first philosophical issue has to do with **space** and is represented in the tradition by Realism and Nominalism. The second has to do with **time** and is represented by what he calls a Transactional and a Processive view. Thus, there are four philosophical options listed, focusing on two daunting philosophical problems, space and time. The following discussion will give a fuller explanation of what is at stake theologically in Rupp's philosophical typology.[27] It must be emphasized that a complete historical account of the four philosophical pressures on theology identified by Rupp, especially Realism and Nominalism, is not possible within the confines of this book. The use of these terms is intended to indicate broad and pervasive philosophical influences on Christology and atonement doctrine, not precise historical instances of that influence.

The philosophical question of space is answered variously by

Realism and Nominalism, according to Rupp's analysis. The question, as it applies to Christology and atonement theory, has to do with the issue of how Christ and/or the work of Christ is applied to human persons as spatial, discreet entities. The second question of time, answered variously by a Transactional or a Processive view considers the issue of when Christ and/or the work of Christ is salvifically effective. It is the question of whether to conceive of the change effected by Christ as accomplished at one time decisively or as the result of development and growth in particular contexts. Each of these philosophical questions and their impact on the formulation of a Christology and atonement theory will now be examined.

One of the essential differences between Realism and Nominalism is the approach to the question of generic, or universal terms. This fundamental philosophical problem influences theology at several key points, especially in the areas of Christology and atonement.

The Realist position with respect to the status of universals advocates the theory that universal, or generic, terms have extra-mental existence. That is, there is something "else" other than discreet individual entities. There is a **universale ante rem**, a universal idea which has non-concrete, but nonetheless real ontological existence apart from the existence of perceivable individual things. Realism, part of Platonism's conceptual content, was the prevailing metaphysical doctrine of the first thousand years of the Christian church's existence and has influenced the early articulation of Christian doctrine.

In Christology and atonement theology, the influence has to do with construing the nature of Christ's humanity and the nature of our humanity and how they are related. Just how the believer gets connected to the saving work and benefits of Christ is not answered univocally in the Christian tradition. The problems which surround this central theological claim, namely, that Christ and the believer are related, connected, or in some way united tend to be further complicated because so few theologies are explicit about the historical and philosophical presuppositions with which they operate. For instance, in B.B. Warfield's typology of atonement theories, he refers to "the so-called mystical theories" which assume that the perfect humanity of Christ somehow purifies humanity's fallen human nature.[28] Warfield identifies much of the Greek Patristic tradition as holding this view and briefly cites a Platonizing influence in the stream of Christian thinking as producing this theory. But Warfield is not explicit about how Platonic and Neoplatonic ideas influenced Christian atonement reflection.

George Rupp is clearer about the specific philosophical issues implied in any given atonement concept. Platonism's doctrine of the real ontological status of general terms shaped a corresponding Christian doctrine of the atonement in ways that emphasized the ontological link between the humanity of Christ (the universal) and particular instantiations of humanity (individual persons). Rupp says that "the conception of universal or generic human nature . . . functions more or less consciously as a cultural presupposition in the patristic and early medieval period to facilitate comprehension of this connection between Christ's work and successive generations of believers."[29]

On Realist metaphysics, Christ's human nature was perceived as a universal.[30] That is, Christ possessed the generic human nature in a way that other human persons do not. Christ, at the Incarnation, took up generic human nature; he took up **Humanity**. Other people are born with a human nature, that is, the set of necessary and sufficient human attributes particular to them, the set of attributes which constitutes their particularity. They reflect or instantiate generic human nature, to be sure, by virtue of the fact that they are human, but they do not **possess** it in an inclusive or defining sense.

Realist-influenced Christology implicitly holds that Jesus Christ's human nature can be conceived as a sort of universal and thus all humanity is, in some way, included in it or instantiations of it. Unlike all other human persons, Jesus Christ possesses the generic human nature in an inclusive sense rather than a participatory sense. Whereas any given human person has a generic human nature, it cannot be said that every human person somehow includes or contains all other human persons. But in the person of Jesus Christ, that can be said. The humanity which Jesus Christ took up at the Incarnation is humanity-at-large, or humanity-as-universal or the Idea of humanity.

Realism influenced the doctrines of the Incarnation and atonement in momentous ways. Soteriological implications are evident in formulating the connection between Christ's salvific work and humanity. How is it that the life, death, and resurrection of this Jesus Christ can be efficacious for any given person? Realism, for many centuries, influenced a theological answer to that question. It implied that there is a fundamental metaphysical connection between Christ and other human individuals, so that Christ's person and the work Christ accomplished accrue naturally to other human persons by virtue of his possessing the generic human nature.

The rise of Nominalism, discernible in the eleventh century, but most marked in the fourteenth, was a profound challenge to some of the most important assumptions of Christian theology, which had been decisively influenced by Realist metaphysics. One of the difficulties in any exposition of Nominalism is that the term itself is difficult to define and a clear advocate difficult to identify.[31] A "radical" Nominalist like Roscelin, condemned at Soissons (A.D. 1092), is a fairly clear example, but "moderate" Nominalists such as Ockham or Abelard are sometimes called Conceptualists or even "moderate" Realists. Thus, careful definition is necessary in delineating the contours of Nominalism.[32]

While conceding all the difficulties of historiography and definition, some general contours of Nominalism and its effect on Christian theology can nonetheless be suggested. The full range of Nominalism's effect on Christian theology cannot be catalogued here; the discussion must be limited to Christological implications.[33] Broadly speaking, Nominalism states that there is nothing other than particular entities; that is, only discreet individual things exist.[34] Abstractable generic concepts are either mere sounds (**flatus vocis**) or, at most, concepts which can refer to individual objects but themselves have no ontological status.

Nominalism can be seen to impact Christology on the view of the relation between the individual person and human nature. Although these lines of influence are complex and mixed with the continuing influence of Realism, some very general contours are discernible.

Because nominalist influenced theology did not posit a universal human nature which Christ uniquely possessed, human persons could no longer naturally participate in the salvific benefits of Christ's person and work. Nominalist influenced theology called into question the fundamental metaphysical connection between Christ's person and work and other human individuals. How persons "get in" on salvation is not by natural inclusion in the unique way in which Christ holds universal human nature but in some other way. Nominalism ultimately gave philosophical support to atonement theories focusing on language of covenant, pact, imputation, and law.[35]

The basic philosophical question concerning space, thus, is answered variously by theologies influenced by Nominalism and Realism. In summary, the question has to do with how the individual person Jesus Christ, spatially located in the first century can have anything to do with an individual human person now, spatially located in the twentieth. Realism's metaphysics influenced theology to answer that question in terms of all human persons being included in the human nature of Christ which has the status of a universal or idea. Nominalism's metaphysics challenged that traditional answer and influenced theology to answer the question in terms, not of ontological union or participation, but in terms of covenant or pact.

The second basic philosophical issue, the temporal issue, can be dealt with briefly. Rupp identifies two options on this issue as well, namely, the Transactional approach and the Processive approach. These two options are not as historically identifiable as Realism and Nominalism. Rupp sees the Transactional approach as primarily the approach of the long tradition of the church and the Processive approach as a latent theme in the tradition but emerging as a recognizable form in the nineteenth century and most recently articulated by Process theology.[36]

These two philosophical options variously influence the answer to the question of "when" the atonement occurred. The transactional view affirms the once-for-all character of the atonement. "The paradigm for the Transactional type is the interpretation which unambiguously and literally affirms the once for all character of the atonement; it understands the work of Christ as effecting a total transformation in the situation of the creation as a whole at the particular historical time of the crucifixion."[37] What happened **then** has salvific impact on humanity **now**.

The Processive approach answers that question by positing the atonement as a process of evolution and change which occurs in each person's own time and context. "As a result, Processive interpretations often emphasize the fact of development and a belief in increase in being and/or value in individual selves, in the cosmic process, or even in God."[38]

This lengthy exposition of Rupp's typology, made necessary by the complexity and importance of the philosophical issues as they relate to theology, further illustrates the thesis that any given atonement typology is constructed in accord to an operating criterion. In Rupp's typology, the criterion is philosophical/historical. He arranges atonement theories according to how they correspond on the philosophical issues of time and space as represented historically and conceptually by Realism/Nominalism and Transaction/Process.

An typology of historical types can be seen in Paul Fiddes' 1989 book, *Past Event and Present Salvation*. Fiddes groups atonement theories according to the relevance of their answers to the pressing questions of each consecutive age in the history of the Church. He identifies the predicament of each particular age as well as the primary metaphor of salvation appropriate to that particular age. He notes,

> Of course, the various ideas of atonement I have listed cannot be confined within the particular historical moments to which I have loosely attached them. They represent responses to types of human experience that can be found in every age; they all, for instance, have some grounding in the New Testament documents. There are periods in human culture where certain images come to the fore and seem relevant, but they persist, overlap and re-form into different combinations, and all express a dimension of human experience that remains valid for us here and now.[39]

There are eight atonement categories, or images of salvation, that

Fiddes has distinguished in the tradition. The first, the New Testament type, sees humanity's predicament as impurity or uncleanness and the main metaphor of salvation as sacrifice, or the cleansing, purifying power of Christ's blood. The second image, typical of the early Church, sees humanity's predicament as enslavement to hostile powers and the main metaphor of salvation as Christ's victory over the powers and the Devil. The third image was also produced in the early Church and shows influence of Greek philosophy. It regards humanity's predicament as the human condition hindering the soul's ascent to God and the corresponding metaphor of salvation as humanity's divinization or ascent in Christ. Next, fourth in line, is the image characteristic of the Middle Ages, which perceives humanity's predicament to be the disturbance of order through sin and the failure of sinners to render God proper honor. The salvific solution to this predicament was captured by the metaphor of Christ settling a debt and restoring order. The fifth image, also appearing in the Middle Ages, was that of courtly love. The predicament of humanity is the loss of love and the metaphor of salvation is that of the cross as a powerful demonstration of the love of God.

The Reformation's perception of humanity's predicament emphasizes the law of God broken by human sin. Salvation, then, in the sixth image, was seen as Christ satisfying the demands of the law of God by substituting for the due punishment of humanity. The seventh image moves to the primary images of the Enlightenment. Humanity's predicament was falling short of the potential of reason, or, ignorance. The corresponding image of salvation was that of Christ influencing the faculties of reason and restoring God-consciousness. Finally, the eighth atonement image is a current one. Fiddes believes that humanity's predicament is perceived in post-Enlightenment modernity as alienation and the image of salvation most accessible to the modern person is one of healing or a restoration of relationships.

These eight images serve as an atonement typology for Fiddes. He attempts, by an historical criterion, to meet the question, "When did this particular salvation motif emerge and what cultural question did it answer?" Fiddes makes no particular claim that one theory is better than any of the others. Although he undoubtedly has his preference, his method of organization is non-polemical and serves instead as an historical/descriptive survey.

Campbell's Objective/Subjective Atonement Theory

The most familiar of all atonement typologies is the objective/subjective classification. As frequent as this typological construction is with respect to atonement theology, it is far from clear what meaning it is meant to convey. Many atonement theologians seem to assume that the content and application of this pair of words is self-evident.

Donald MacKinnon has suggested a definition of the terms that is helpful. He says that an objective atonement theory is one that focuses or concentrates on the accomplishment of a verdict on the human scene.[40] A subjective theory is one which focuses or concentrates on the manner in which the individual makes the work of Christ his or her own.[41] It is critical to note that MacKinnon does not in any way set these two types of theories in opposition to one another. They emphasize different aspects of the work of Christ but are not mutually exclusive.

George Hendry defines objective/subjective similarly to MacKinnon. A subjective interpretation "sees salvation as a change in consciousness" and an objective interpretation, somewhat circuitously stated, stresses "the objectivity of the atonement. . . a transformation of the human situation that is objectively real prior to our consciousness of it. . ."[42]

David Wells points out that the objective/subjective typology deals with one of the main questions about the atonement, namely, "whether the atonement was completed in Christ's own time in history or whether it is reenacted in subsequent human life in some way."[43] An objective theory of the atonement concentrates primarily on the fact of the past event of Christ's saving work. It is accomplished; it is a once-for-all decisive past event; it is done completely independently of our individual participation and awareness. A subjective theory of the atonement concentrates primarily on the present experience or awareness of being reconciled to God.

Although it is not blind to the historical events of the life and death of Jesus Christ, it finds the salvific significance of Jesus Christ in the present, not in the past.

Ingolf Dalferth emphasizes the primacy of the objective foundations of atonement reflection when he points out the fallacy of the fact/interpretation model applied to atonement. He says that Christians do not take the objective historical event of Jesus Christ's death and change it into a subjective soteriological event by reflecting theologically upon it. "The soteriological understanding of Christ's death is not a secondary soteriological interpretation of a primary unsoteriological understanding of Jesus' death and resurrection. . ." [44] Rather, "The saving significance of Christ's death does not follow; it precedes everything we believe, think, or do."

A basic understanding of the terms objective and subjective, on the basis of the definitions of the theologians surveyed above, is one of temporal reference. An objective account **locates** the decisive work of the atonement in the past, in the events surrounding the life, death, and resurrection of Jesus Christ. A subjective account **locates** the decisive work of the atonement in the present, in the individual's here-and-now acceptance and participation in the significance of those past events.

In addition, an objective account identifies God as the primary actor in the atonement. It is God who initiates, accomplishes, and guarantees the atonement. Human persons are involved, to be sure, but an objective account stresses the divine origin and efficacy of the atonement.

Other theologians would rather avoid these vexed terms of objective and subjective altogether. G.W.H. Lampe feels there is little utility left in words that display such a cluster of philosophical and epistemological difficulties. He explains some of the problems,

I prefer to avoid the term "objective" in speaking of the Atonement, partly because of its obvious philosophical difficulties and partly because many theologians have assumed that the death of Christ can have objective efficacy only if it is an act directed either towards God, in satisfaction of his justice or in somehow making it possible for his love to operate for the forgiveness of sinners without compromising his holiness, or towards a personal devil in somehow liberating sinners from his clutches. I should wish, on the contrary, to say that the objective efficacy of the death of Christ lies in it being an act of God Incarnate directed towards man, placing him in a new relation to himself by a decisive act of acceptance.[45]

In response to this statement by G.W.H. Lampe, Donald MacKinnon emphasizes, ". . . I would wish to speak of the act of God in Christ as objective, as something built into the structure of the world, even perhaps (as I think Barth would agree) its very foundation."[46] This accent is echoed as well by Leonard Hodgson, who sees definite positive value in a subjective account but is sure that the objective focus on "something accomplished, something done," is absolutely critical for a theory of the Atonement.[47]

The most important interpretation of objective and subjective has to do with the **locus** and **source** of the decisive salvific event. An objective account places primary, but not necessarily exclusive, salvific emphasis on the life, death, and resurrection of Jesus of Nazareth in the first century. A subjective account places primary, but not necessarily exclusive, salvific emphasis on the appropriation of reconciliation with God in the consciousness of the individual in the individual's own time.[48]

John McLeod Campbell understood clearly that an atonement theology can be adequate only if it includes both objective and subjective elements. He said in a 1853 letter to Thomas Erskine that, ". . . all spiritual occupation with the **objective**, in regard to the sacrifice of Christ, must **imply** the **subjective**, and thus participation in the death of Christ **underlies** the confidence towards God with which that death is contemplated. . ."[49] Campbell knew from the experiences of his ministry at Row that it was a truncated, fearful faith which concentrated only on the objective, once-for-all fact of Christ's sacrifice and did not subsequently issue in full confidence and acceptance as well-loved children of God.

In line with his own Reformed tradition, Campbell placed the primary locus of salvation in the life, death, and resurrection of Jesus

Christ and the sole source of atoning effect in the divine purpose or intent. In this, he is an objective atonement theorist. But he also, and emphatically, urged his listeners and readers to participate in the life of Christ, to know with assurance their salvation, to be confident of the love of the Father. In fact, he insists that it is only in the effects of the atonement in the lives of people that the meaning of the atonement can be understood at all. In this, he inserts a strong dose of subjective elements in his atonement theology. It is the combination of these two elements which produces the complete and balanced atonement theology of John McLeod Campbell.

Because of this satisfying balance of elements, Campbell does not fit conveniently into either an objective or subjective category. In spite of the efforts of a number of interpreters to force his theology on to a Procrustean bed of the objective/subjective scheme, it manages to resist such attempts and draw new inquirers and admirers.[50]

Some of what Campbell says does lead to conflicting interpretations. Because he emphasizes the superiority of an understanding of the atonement which springs from a full confidence in the love of God rather than a fearful apprehension of whether God loves us and because he attempts to right the balance of Westminster federal theology, he sometimes sounds decidedly subjective: ". . . the superiority of a moral and spiritual atonement, consisting in the right response from humanity to the divine mind in relation to sin, becomes clear."[51] But this feature of Campbell's theology is meant to be corrective of previous bad theology rather than as indicative of an atonement theory with little regard for the salvation won for us by Christ in an actual time and place.

Although Campbell is certainly aware of the objective and subjective elements in his atonement theology, he chooses to employ different terminology to structure his theory. The retrospective/ prospective scheme by which Campbell unfolds his atonement theology is more effective than the objective/subjective scheme because it highlights the complete inter-relatedness of the objective event's impact on the subjective faith experience of the believer. For Campbell, the response of Christ to the Father in relation to our sins was the heart of the redemptive act. That can be considered the objective event. But it is only as we participate in that same response which Christ made that our status as beloved children of God can be realized and actualized. Campbell says that, "we must partake in it (Christ's response to the Father), and must have its elements reproduced in us. . ."[52] Objective and subjective elements of the atonement cannot be extracted and examined independently of each other. They are completely and irretrievably united.

Each aspect of the retrospective and each aspect of the prospective has, in Campbell's account, both objective content and subjective implications. The retrospective aspect, that is, the focus on the remission of sins, has the objective content of Christ's perfectly witnessing the love of the Father and Christ perfectly confessing humanity's sin to the Father. But those two objective events have immediate subjective application. It is only in the believer's full assurance of the Father's love and the believer's participation in the perfect confession of Christ that the retrospective aspect of the atonement is complete and whole. Likewise, the prospective aspect, that is, the focus on the promise of eternal life, has the objective content of Christ displaying the life of sonship and Christ's continual intercession for humanity before the Father. But, again, those objective events have subjective implications that cannot be separated from the objective content. For the believer is a part of the prospective aspect; the believer finds her authentic redeemed identity in the life of sonship and the believer joins in intercession with Christ through the acts of worship and praise.

Thus, it can be seen that Campbell bursts the boundaries of the objective/subjective classification. His concept of the atonement as retrospective and prospective is a suggestive and creative addition to the objective/subjective atonement theory classification. Because Campbell succeeds in thoroughly integrating the objective and subjective, the result is a dynamic atonement account that highlights the connections, relations, and implications of the work of the Christ with the response of the believer.

NOTES

1. John Macquarrie, *Jesus Christ in Modern Thought* (London: SCM Press, 1990), p. 400.

2. In his book on the atonement Dillistone makes this point as well, "It is fundamental to the whole thesis of this book that reconciliation between God and man, man and God, cannot be expressed through any single shape or pattern." Cf. F.W. Dillistone, *The Christian Understanding of Atonement* (Philadelphia: Westminster Press, 1968), p. 410.

3. Hastings Rashdall, *The Idea of Atonement in Christian Theology* (London: Macmillan, 1920), p. 420.

4. The briefest perusal of Rashdall's book will yield numerous more vigorous invectives against objective theories. Cf. p. 428 and p. 360. For rebuttals of Rashdall, cf. Alister McGrath, "The Moral Theory of the Atonement: An Historical and Theological Critique," *Scottish Journal of Theology* 38 (1985), pp. 205-220.

5. Rashdall, *The Idea of Atonement in Christian Theology*, p. 425.

6. This particular task will be taken up in the following section.

7. Gustaf Aulen, *Christus Victor: An Historical Study of the Three Main Types of the Idea of the Atonement* (New York: Macmillan Publishing Co., 1969).

8. George Rupp, *Christologies and Cultures, Toward a Typology of Religious Worldviews* (The Hague: Mouton & Co., 1974), p. 17 ff.

9. Other critical voices of Aulen include Paul Fiddes, *Past Event and Present Salvation*, p. 27.

10. They are found on pp. 356-369 in Benjamin Breckinridge Warfield, *The Person and Work of Christ* (Philadelphia: The Presbyterian and Reformed Publishing Company, 1950).

11. *The Person and Work of Christ*, p. 356.

12. Bernard and Luther, respectively.

13. Warfield, *The Person and Work of Christ*, p. 359.

14. Whether Warfield is entirely correct both in his identification of this theory and his examples of the theory's promoters is an important question.

15. Warfield's own view of the Rectoral theory is scarcely concealed when he says, "When the Calvinism of the New England Puritans began to break down, one of the symptoms of its decay was the gradual substitution of the rectoral for the satisfaction view of the Atonement." *The Person and Work of Christ*, p. 364.

16. *The Person and Work of Christ*, p. 366.

17. *The Person and Work of Christ*, p. 367. This remark is directed also at R.C. Moberly's account, which Warfield mistakenly takes to be equivalent to Campbell's.

18. Warfield, *The Person and Work of Christ*, p. 368.

19. David Wells, in his book *Search for Salvation* (Leicester, England: Inter Varsity Press, 1978), p. 10, makes a similar point about atonement typologies when he says that "the underlying presuppositions in the various theological schemes are not always recognized and seldom ever aired, yet it is on these presuppositions that almost everything turns."

20. Dillistone's book is important because it is learned, thorough, imaginative, and fully aware of the multiple complexities of atonement theology. Furthermore, because it impressively incorporates poetry, music, psychology, and literature, the book is a fine example of a theological endeavor which harvests the bounty of many disciplines. It is puzzling because Dillistone's curious blend of Hegelianism and existentialism is always present, although usually this emerges in introductory comments before he embarks on his consistently excellent historical-theological survey of each motif under question.

An example of Dillistone's Hegelianism is evident in this short passage: "The soul of the universe, it is imaged, breathes out and breathes in, gathers itself up into an ecstasy of life, retreats again into the womb of death. In its beginning is its end: in its end is its beginning. In the thesis is the antithesis: in the antithesis the thesis is renewed" (p. 410). An example of Dillistone's existentialism may be recounted as follows: "Sometimes vaguely, sometimes poignantly, sometimes resignedly, sometimes rebelliously, man clings to his life and its extensions, hugs it to himself, strives to preserve it at all costs. Yet in the very clinging there is a sense of being out of harmony with the essential rhythm of life. And once the rhythm is broken, man seems to lurch forward to the point of no return" (p. 411).

21. *The Christian Understanding of Atonement*, p. 27.

22. Dillistone, *The Christian Understanding of Atonement*, p. 27.

23. *The Christian Understanding of Atonement*, p. 27. The reason why Dillistone calls the models of corporate experience "analogues" and the models of individual experience "parables" is unclear.

24. Dillistone, *The Christian Understanding of Atonement*, p. 27.

25. Dillistone does admit in the conclusion to his book that the eight images attempt to "cover the main aspects of human life" but that "life cannot be parcelled up as neatly as this (group of images) may suggest. There are bound to be overlappings and mergings of symbols and images." *The Christian Understanding of Atonement*, p. 406.

26. George Rupp, *Christologies and Cultures; Toward a Typology of Religious Worldviews*, p. 27. Rupp rightly notes, "In classifying a thinker's approach to interpreting the significance of Christ one is, then, also describing his at least implicit metaphysics" (p. 48).

27. A lengthy explication of the philosophical issues raised by Rupp is warranted for this study in that some of these issues appear prominently in Campbell's atonement theology.

28. Warfield, *The Person and Work of Christ*, pp. 355-357.

29. Rupp, *Christologies and Cultures*, p. 38.

30. Conciliar creeds or particular treatises by early theologians need not explicitly use the language of universals in order for this general line or approach to be evident.

31. Alister McGrath, "Homo Assumptus?: A Study in the Christology of the **Via Moderna**, with Particular Reference to William of Ockham," *Ephemerides Theologicae Lovaniensis* 60 (1984), p. 283.

32. Alister McGrath surveys the difficulties of identification and definition surrounding Nominalism. Cf. *The Intellectual Origins of the European Reformation* (Oxford: Blackwell Publishers, 1987), pp. 70-74.

33. Nominalism influenced the doctrine of God in decisive ways as well. The distinction between the *potentia absoluta* and the *potentia ordinaria* was momentous for the doctrine of the decrees of God, election and predestination and subsequent covenant theology. These issues lie outside the scope of this survey.

34. Rupp, *Christologies and Cultures*, p. 34.

35. This is not to say that atonement theologies employing metaphors of imputation are, by definition, nominalist. But the use of such metaphors can be seen as an influence of Nominalism.

36. Rupp identifies Irenaeus' recapitulation theory as an example of a Processive approach from early in the tradition, cf. *Christologies and Cultures*, p. 73.

37. Rupp, *Christologies and Cultures*, p. 46.

38. *Christologies and Cultures*, p. 46.

39. Paul S. Fiddes, *Past Event and Present Salvation; The Christian Idea of Atonement*, p. 12.

40. Donald MacKinnon, "The Conflict between Realism and Idealism," *Explorations in Theology 5* (London: SCM Press, Ltd., 1979), p. 158.

41. MacKinnon, "The Conflict between Realism and Idealism," p. 158.

42. George Hendry, *The Gospel of the Incarnation* (Philadelphia: Westminster Press, 1958), p. 130, 131.

43. Personal correspondence, July 14, 1991.

44. Ingolf U. Dalferth, "Christ Died for Us: Reflections on the Sacrificial Language of Salvation," from *Sacrifice and Redemption: Durham Essay in Theology*, ed. Stephen W. Sykes (Cambridge: Cambridge University Press, 1991), p. 316.

45. G.W.H. Lampe and D.M. MacKinnon, *The Resurrection, A Dialogue* (Philadelphia: Westminster Press, 1966), p. 100.

46. Lampe and MacKinnon, *The Resurrection*, p. 110.

47. Leonard Hodgson, *The Doctrine of the Atonement* (New York: Charles Scribner's Sons, 1951), p. 83.

48. B.B. Warfield's definition of an objective atonement theory does not explicitly use a temporal referent or clearly indicate divine initiative and thus serves as a good example of the diversity, even confusion, which surrounds this term. For Warfield, an objective account is a "God-ward" account. That is, an atonement theory must clearly refer to the work of Christ as "terminating" on God in order to qualify as an objective account. Cf. *The Person and Work of Christ*, p. 364. The word "terminating" is Warfield's expression. Synonyms may be "impacting" or "affecting."

Warfield's rather cryptic definition of an objective atonement theory is not so much a definition as a vote for a particular atonement metaphor. Warfield's clear preference in atonement theories is the penal substitutionary metaphor which explicitly holds that the work of Christ "terminates" on God primarily. This preference strongly influences his perception of an objective atonement theory.

49. *Memorials*, vol. 1, p. 249. Emphasis Campbell's.

50. The wide variety of interpretive response to Campbell's atonement theology has already been noted. A few examples of interpreters of Campbell who criticize his theory for its subjectivity include George Carey, now Archbishop of Canterbury, who says that "Campbell evacuates the atonement of any 'objective' content. . . We have here, incidentally, a variation of the 'moral influence' theory . . ." George Carey, *The Gate of Glory* (London: Hodder and Stoughton, 1986), p. 30. Robert S. Paul also calls Campbell's view a variant of the Moral Theory, one largely vacated of an historical referent. Robert S. Paul, *The Atonement and the Sacraments* (New York: Abingdon Press, 1960), p. 147.

Then there are the interpreters of Campbell who warmly praise Campbell for his subjective, moral-influence theory of salvation. Cf. Eugene Bewkes, p. 285.

Others, however, see an objective atonement theorist in John McLeod Campbell. An appreciative account of Campbell comes from J.H. Leckie in a review of *The Nature of the Atonement*, an account which specifically claims Campbell's atonement theology to be in the line of objective theories. J.H. Leckie, "John McLeod Campbell's 'The Nature of the Atonement'," *The Expository Times* 40 (1929), 198-204. A more recent article on Campbell affirms strong continuity between Anselm, commonly considered the most objective of all atonement theorists, and Campbell. Whatever differences exists between Campbell and Anselm, this article claims, are peripheral and not central or determinative. Trevor A. Hart, "Anselm of Canterbury and

John McLeod Campbell: Where Opposites Meet?," *The Evangelical Quarterly* 62 (1990), 211-333.

51. *The Nature of the Atonement*, p. 184.

52. *The Nature of the Atonement*, p. 295.

CHAPTER FOUR

DIFFICULTIES IN CAMPBELL'S ATONEMENT THEOLOGY

John McLeod Campbell's complex, yet balanced, atonement theology has met with a variety of responses and critical evaluations. Some of the negative critiques have been based on misunderstandings of Campbell's terminology or a confusion of categories. Some of the positive responses verge on effusive admiration of, not careful attention to, this pastor/theologian who spoke and wrote so consistently of the gracious love of God. Careful, judicious evaluation of Campbell's atonement theology confronts several difficulties, briefly identified at the end of chapter two. These difficulties have to do with the nature of Christ's sufferings, the perfect confession of Christ, and the relationship of Christ with human persons. This chapter will attempt to examine carefully each of these problems in Campbell's theology with the intent to confirm the consistency and coherence of Campbell's overall account. The chapter will demonstrate that the unique interpretive difficulties of Campbell's theory are not, in the end, insurmountable. In fact, most of the problems surrounding these three issues in Campbell's theory can be traced to misunderstandings of key Campbell terms.

The Nature of Christ's Sufferings

Campbell's discussion on the sufferings of Christ in *The Nature of the Atonement* raise two interpretive issues, the issue of whether Christ's sufferings were real and the issue of whether Christ's sufferings were penal in nature. Some interpreters, responding to the first issue, see in Campbell's theory of Christ's sufferings a docetic tendency.[1] Responding to the second issue, others object to Campbell's view of Christ's sufferings because they insist these sufferings must be penal in nature and they correctly see in Campbell a firm rejection of the sufferings-as-punishment idea.[2]

In explicating Campbell's view of the sufferings of Christ, it is first necessary to examine the atonement theories of the Calvinist tradition which Campbell finds objectionable. These objectionable views are held, in Campbell's terms, by the "elder Calvinists" and "modified Calvinism" and summarized by Campbell in chapters three and four of *The Nature of the Atonement*. It is important to grasp the approach of Campbell's predecessors in order to understand Campbell's view more completely.

Campbell believes the tradition of Calvinism had gone wrong in its doctrine of the atonement because important first principles were ignored or muted. The first principles he has in mind, characteristically, are that God is love and that God is the gracious Father of his adopted children. On this basis, Campbell targets both the elder Calvinists with their penal substitution view of the atonement and the federal, or "modified," Calvinists with their rectoral justice view of the atonement. These two options in the Calvinist stream are represented in Campbell's book by John Owen, Jonathan Edwards, and Thomas Chalmers for the older Calvinist position and George Payne, Ralph Wardlaw, Thomas Jenkyn, and John Pye Smith for the federalists.

Campbell's grouping of Owen, Edwards, and Chalmers as representative of one discrete form of Calvinism is most peculiar. These three theologians are highly individual; their contexts are distinct; their concerns and influences are very different. Each represents a different century, country, temperament, and theology. John Owen (1616-83) was a seventeenth century British Puritan theologian and statesmen living in England during the frequently violent years of Cromwell and the Restoration. Jonathan Edwards (1703-58) was an eighteenth century American frontier preacher, theologian, and philosopher during the years of the Great Awakening. Thomas Chalmers (1780-1847) was a moderate Calvinist Presbyterian churchman in early nineteenth century Scotland, most remembered for his evangelical preaching and his involvement in the Secession of 1834.

Yet Campbell chose to present these three as Calvinists whose "theology is one."[3] Perhaps Campbell was not fully aware of the many important theological differences between Owen, Edwards, and Chalmers.[4] Or, more likely, Campbell was interested in contrasting his own atonement theology with previous options in the Reformed tradition. A complete comparison was not his intent. Historical sensitivity and conceptual accuracy was not the main concern. Rather, he wished to make a point about atonement options in the Reformed tradition and chose three representative, although diverse, voices to represent a particular view. Although Campbell's intent was most likely pedagogical in grouping together Owen, Edwards, and Chalmers, that is, to lift up the common feature of a penal substitutionary view, it must be emphasized that these voices are so distinct with respect to many aspects of the atonement that Campbell's grouping of them here into one unit is helpful only in a most general way. This first stream, then, combines several Calvinist variations, including the Puritan tradition, high Presbyterianism, and the highly distinctive, not easily definable voice of Jonathan Edwards.[5]

The second stream identified by Campbell is more specific. He chose to represent the tradition of federal theology or covenant theology with the obscure names of Pye Smith, Payne, Jenkyn, and Wardlaw.[6] The focus here is the notion of Christ's satisfaction as modified by federal theology. In contrast to orthodox Calvinism's view of Christ's sufferings as an exact equivalent to the penalty of sin due to human sinners, federal theologians modified the theory to state that Christ's sufferings were not punishment for sin but rather sufferings which make the forgiveness of God consistent to and supportive of a proper moral order. That is, the atonement does not literally pay the debt of human sin but it renders the forgiveness of God plausible and fitting for the good government of a moral universe.

John Pye Smith, one of the federalists Campbell refers to, defines the atonement in classic federalist terms. "Atonement, therefore, or Reconciliation, or Satisfaction, is a provision for guarding the laws of eternal wisdom; so that the goodness of the Divine Government may sustain no disparagement, in receiving transgressors to favour and in conferring upon them the richest benefits of benevolence." Again, Pye Smith reveals his federalist framework when he insists that a study of the sacrifice of Christ must be preceded by, ". . . attention to the nature, reasons, and moral operation of a compensative arrangement, by which the restoration of the sinner may be effected without detriment to the public righteousness of the Most High."[7]

Campbell finds this modified theory nearly as objectionable as penal substitution.[8] The "axiomatic defect" of both systems is that they conceive of the atonement as a legal transaction rather than the establishment of a filial relationship.[9]

Campbell's objections to the two systems outlined above come to sharpest focus in his reflections on the sufferings of Christ. The root of all of Campbell's dissatisfaction with the Calvinist tradition is the predominantly legal metaphors and conceptual framework of the doctrine of the atonement. This legal terminology also affected language on the sufferings of Christ. In the view of the older Calvinists, Christ's sufferings, made possible by his divinity, were an equivalent punishment to the deserved penalty for human sin. The concept was one of numerical or quantitative equivalence. In the view of the federal Calvinists, Christ's sufferings were not an equivalent punishment but rather a means, or instrument, to restore the balance of God's proper moral government of the universe. The divinity of Christ, on this view, gave infinite value and dignity to the sufferings.

Consonant with Campbell's theology as a whole, he insists that the sufferings of Christ "arose **naturally** out of what He was, and the relation in which He stood to those for whose sins he suffered. . ."[10] Christ's divinity did not either make possible or give adequate weight and dignity to Christ's sufferings. Rather, Christ's sufferings were the outward form of the holiness and love of Christ. The sufferings were not punishment. They were a demonstration of, or the visible manifestation of, the primary attribute and motivation of God, namely, love. In other words, when the believer looks at the sufferings of Christ, the believer ought not to see the punishment of a wrathful God. Rather, the believer ought to see in Christ's sufferings God's love and mercy. Campbell puts it succinctly, ". . .

while Christ suffered for our sins as an atoning sacrifice, what he suffered was not - because from its nature it could not be - a punishment."[11]

Campbell finds in Jonathan Edwards a support of this view of the sufferings of Christ.[12] Although Edwards is, for Campbell, an example of the older Calvinism, a view Campbell rejects, he also serves to reinforce Campbell on certain points. Perhaps it can be said that this dual role of Edwards in Campbell's argument illustrates Campbell's high regard for Edwards; Campbell, it seems, was eager here, and periodically throughout his book, to find in the esteemed Edwards a voice of affirmation and support for his argument.

In stating so clearly his aversion to the idea of Christ's sufferings as punishment, Campbell makes a crucial distinction between atonement and substituted punishment. The Calvinist tradition, in both the "older" and the "modified" forms that Campbell identified, **equated** the atonement with penal substitution. That is, according to Campbell's reading of the Calvinist tradition, atonement **is** substituted punishment. The atonement was effectuated in that Christ suffered as substitute for the punishment due sinful humanity. It is this concept that Campbell rejects. He does so by distinguishing between the essence of the atonement and the fact of Christ's sufferings.

Far from being parallel or synonymous concepts, the atonement and Christ's sufferings refer to quite different realities. Christ's sufferings are, as stated above, the visible manifestations of the foundational love and mercy of God. They are the "form of holiness and love under the pressure of our sin," as Campbell puts it. The atonement is effected not through the sufferings of Christ but through the perfect witness of Christ to the Father and the perfect confession of human sin by Christ to the Father, concepts that will be further considered below. The atonement, Campbell stresses, is not punishment; it is the whole gracious activity of God in Christ, rooted in the desire of divine love, bridging the alienation between God and God's lost children. Thus, Christ's sufferings are actually illustrations or demonstrations of God's motivation in the atonement. Campbell's view of the sufferings of Christ are as far removed as possible from the idea of God punishing Christ as a substitute or pouring out his wrath accumulated in the face of persistent human sin.

Although Campbell clearly and unambiguously distances himself from the idea that Christ's sufferings were a punishment, it is not as clear and unambiguous what his own view is, that the sufferings are a "form of holiness and love." Thus, it is necessary to explore further Campbell's reflections on Christ's sufferings.

It will be recalled that Campbell divides his atonement theory into the retrospective aspect and the prospective aspect and each of these into a direction toward God and a direction toward humanity. Discussion on the suffering of Christ fits in primarily in the first big division of Campbell's atonement theology, the retrospective aspect. More specifically, Campbell first examines the suffering of Christ as it functions in the atonement's direction toward humanity of the retrospective aspect. That is, he examines first how Christ's sufferings function in the atonement as the remission of sins (retrospective) from the perspective of how Christ represented the Father to humanity.

Because Christ was a witness, or a representative, for the Father to humanity, and because that witness was a "living epistle of the grace of God," Christ met with hostility, enmity, and hatred.[13] On account of that, he suffered. Campbell says,

> "His honouring of the Father caused men to dishonour Him, - His manifestation of brotherly love was repaid with hatred, - His perfect walk in the sight of men failed to commend either His Father or Himself, - His professed trust in the Father was cast up to Him, not being believed, and the bitter complaint was wrung from Him - 'reproach hath broken my heart.' "[14]

But this suffering which Christ experienced in that he came as a gracious witness to humanity of the Father was not a threat or hindrance to Christ's witness-bearing of the Father. Rather, Christ's sufferings were a perfection or enhancement of that witness. Campbell's point is in contrast to the Calvinist traditions he is attempting to correct. Instead of construing the sufferings as a punishment for humanity's sin, Campbell wishes to construe the sufferings as a perfect and necessary part of Christ's witnessing for the Father to humanity.[15] That is, when the believer sees the suffering Christ, the believer sees more fully the loving and forgiving heart of the Father. The core of Campbell's conviction here is that the sufferings of Christ are not a punishment from God but actually a revelation of the heart of God.[16]

Christ was able to endure these sufferings because of his unshakable confidence in the Father's love.[17] Here emerges one of the most interesting exegetical moves that Campbell makes to support his point. Not even the cry of dereliction, traditionally interpreted to mean Christ's utter loneliness and forsakenness on the cross, can indicate a separation between the Father and the Son. In fact, according to Campbell, the cry of dereliction actually is a shout of confidence and trust. Campbell believes that the interpreter of this part of the passion narrative must consider all of Psalm 22, not just the first words which Christ uttered. In saying, "My God, my God, why have you forsaken me?" Christ really had in mind the entire psalm, a psalm of confidence and assurance in the faithfulness of God. Campbell explains,

> The character of this psalm as a whole is, therefore, quite unequivocal, viz. a dealing of the Father with Christ in which the cup of man's enmity is drank by Him to its last drop, in the experience of absolute weakness . . . But trust in God, personal trust, is that of which the trial is most conspicuous as pervading the psalm . . . trust which the Father permits to be thus tried; but trust the root of which in the Father's favour has not been cut off, not even touched by any act of the Father or expression of His face as if He were turned into an enemy. . .[18]

Campbell is further convinced that only such a reading of the cry of dereliction is consonant with several other words from the cross, specifically, "Father, forgive them," and "Into your hands I commend my spirit."[19] Most importantly, this reading of the passion narrative strengthens Campbell's foundational principle that the love of God supports and motivates the entire framework of the atonement, in all its constitutive parts.

By this reading of the cry of dereliction, it is clear that Campbell wishes to safeguard and highlight the filial trust between the Father and the Son. He wishes, further, to assure fearful people of God's unrelenting and unequivocal love for them, no matter what the circumstances.[20] But in his desire to purchase these truths, Campbell may have paid a high price. He seems not to consider the alternate idea that even if Christ experienced utter desolation and forsakenness in the cry of dereliction, God was still with him in a final, though hidden, sense. He seems not to realize that to deny the absolute loneliness of Christ's experience on the cross is, implicitly, to suggest that Christ cannot really be with us in our moments of absolute loneliness. For only a Christ who has experienced the darkest valley of the shadow of death can truly walk with us through our dark and forsaken valleys.[21]

Further explication of the sufferings of Christ emerge in Campbell's discussion of the second part of the retrospective aspect, namely, Christ's dealing with the Father on behalf of humanity. Here the suffering results not because Christ as the perfect witness of the Father experiences the "constant pressure" of sin, but rather because Christ, as mediator on behalf of humanity, experiences fully the wrath of God concerning sin.[22] By this Campbell does not mean penal suffering or the suffering of a punishment poured out by God. He means that in this mediatorial role of the retrospective aspect, Christ was "meeting the divine mind in its aspect towards sin and sinners" and Christ was "dealing with the righteous wrath of God against sin, interposing Himself between sinners and the consequences of that righteous wrath. . ."[23]

It is important to note that Campbell's argument with the tradition is not over the reality of God's wrath against sin. He is not adverse to using the language of divine wrath and expiation of sin.[24] But Campbell is convinced the tradition has gone wrong in the conception of how that divine wrath was to be appeased. Christ did give "satisfaction" to the righteous demands of God; that satisfaction, though, has nothing to do with substituted punishment.[25]

At this point, one of the most difficult and controversial of Campbell's atonement concepts emerges. So clearly does Campbell reject the idea of substituted punishment as a means of satisfying the righteous demands of God and meeting the divine wrath of God, that an entirely different concept must take its place. That concept, for Campbell, is Christ's perfect confession of our sins and is introduced in the famous sentence, "This confession, as to its own nature, must have been **a perfect Amen in humanity to the judgment of God on the sin of man**."[26] That is, Christ, in his divine humanity, perfectly acknowledged, experienced, and affirmed the wrath, judgement, and sorrow of God over sin. He was in "responsive unity" with the Father concerning sin.[27] Christ's perfect confession on behalf of all humanity entailed suffering in that suffering was a natural, or inescapable, response of "the divine holiness and divine love in humanity to the aspect of the divine mind in the Father towards the sins of men."[28] Suffering gave "ultimate depth" to Christ's confession of humanity's sin; it signaled or guaranteed the full realization in Christ's spirit of sin's scandal in God's eyes.[29]

So, both the God-ward and the humanity-ward directions of the retrospective aspect involve suffering on the part of Christ, each for a different reason. The humanity-ward direction emphasizes the **humanity** of Christ; suffering came in that Christ's perfect witnessing for the Father was rejected and scorned.[30] The God-ward direction emphasizes the **divinity** of Christ; the divinity-in-humanity of Christ recoiled from sin and suffered in a full knowledge of how the Father reacts to human sin. These alternate emphases on the humanity and the divinity of Christ are not hard and fast divisions; Campbell assumes the **unity** of the person of the Redeemer. But Campbell places a slightly different emphasis on the **divine**-humanity and the divine-**humanity** of Christ with respect to Christ's sufferings.[31]

The above exposition of the sufferings of Christ in Campbell's atonement theology demonstrates the function and purpose of the sufferings in the overall atonement scheme. It has been noted that the sufferings occupy a primary place in the retrospective aspect, or, the remission of sins.

But Campbell has more to say about the sufferings of Christ. Near the end of his book, he devotes two full chapters to the sufferings of Christ, trying yet again to come to terms with this most difficult problem.[32] When Campbell broke the equation of atonement and substituted punishment, he took on the burden of accounting for the sufferings of Christ in a way that does not render them gratuitous. Although Campbell does not say as much, it seems by the additional lengthy exposition of the sufferings of Christ near the end of his book that he is well aware of this burden.

Pressing any atonement theology at this precise point always raises the most difficult questions, questions which range from issues of theodicy to Christology to pastoral care. Why did Christ have to suffer? Why did God allow Christ to suffer? How is it that we are saved through a suffering Christ? What does suffering mean for us today? Campbell answers these questions by focusing on the nature of Christ's sufferings as a natural result of a sinful world and on their unique ability to witness to God's love and forgiveness. But when he tries to answer the root question, "But why was all this suffering necessary?" he resorts to the secret mysteries of the divine counsel. "In accomplishing these results, we have now seen that, in order to the perfection of the work of Christ as witnessing for God to men, **it has appeared to the divine wisdom necessary** to subject His love and trust towards the Father, and His long-suffering forgiveness in bearing the contradiction of sinners against Himself, to the trial of the hour and power of darkness."[33]

Campbell is consistent in his extended reflections on the sufferings of Christ. He insists that Christ's sufferings are a revelation of the love and mercy of God, that they never broke Christ's confidence in the Father's favor and love, that they are a part of the whole sacrifice of Christ.[34] He also insists that Christ's sufferings call the believing community to a fellowship in Christ's sufferings, a sharing in Christ's sufferings and a call to discipleship.[35] Furthermore, he continues to maintain that the sufferings should not be construed as a punishment of God, a separation of God, or a sign of God's displeasure.[36]

Campbell's reflections on the sufferings of Christ have been dealt with at some length because they offer the clearest example of Campbell's distance from and rejection of a main element in the Calvinist tradition. So convinced was he that the whole concept of penal substitution was axiomatically defective that he recast the entire discussion of Christ's sufferings into the framework of Christ's full trust and confidence in God. The sufferings, far from a punishment, were actually a revelation of the love of God, a disclosure of the seriousness of sin, and a sign of Christ's oneness with the Father. By radically changing the idea of Christ's sufferings, though, Campbell does not leave the question of how salvation is actually effected unanswered. When he broke the equation between penal substitution and atonement, he replaced it with the alternative he discovered in Jonathan Edwards, namely, that an adequate confession of sin could also satisfy the justice of God and result in atonement. It is to this fascinating, puzzling, and problematic, idea that we now turn.

The Confession of Christ

Campbell's aversion to penal substitution led him not only to recast thinking concerning Christ's sufferings but also to introduce the striking idea of Christ's confession or repentance as the heart of the atonement. Introduced and summarized by Campbell with an unusually incisive sentence, "This confession as to its own nature must have been a **perfect Amen in humanity to the judgment of God on the sin of man**,"[37] this idea has been both roundly dismissed and routinely misunderstood by Campbell interpreters. This section will demonstrate that, although this concept has its attendant theological, conceptual and Scriptural difficulties, it is a promising and serious atonement contribution and one which, if taken in the context of Campbell's full atonement theory, avoids many of the charges levelled against it.

Campbell's reflections on Christ's confession, as stated in chapter two above, came from a suggestion in a treatise of Jonathan Edwards.[38] Edwards stated briefly that "either an equivalent punishment or an equivalent sorrow and repentance" could sufficiently meet the justice requirements of a holy God. Quickly dismissing the second option, Edwards maintained the traditional Calvinist doctrine of penal substitution. It was this option, bypassed by Edwards, that intrigued Campbell and led him to formulate his doctrine of the perfect confession of Christ.

Because Campbell so decisively repudiated the doctrine of substituted punishment as the center of the atoning work of Christ, an alternate conception of how it is that Christ dealt with sin and its affront to the holiness of God was necessary. The doctrine of penal substitution, although it had difficulty making convincing the love of God, nonetheless, rather dramatically explained the necessity of the sufferings and death of Christ, that is, they were necessary to avert the punishment properly belonging to humanity. The challenge facing Campbell, in his alternate concept of Christ's perfect confession, was to make equally convincing the necessity of the sufferings and death of Christ. For if Christ's sufferings and death were seen as somehow superfluous or extraneous, Campbell's atonement theology would and should be charged with coherence and justice problems every bit as problematic as the penal substitution theory it was intended to replace.

In the discussion in the section above of Campbell's reflections on the sufferings of Christ it was demonstrated that this challenge to make necessary and important the sufferings and death of Christ has already partly been met. The sufferings of Christ were not, Campbell insisted, substituted punishment. They were, rather, a revelation of the love of God, a disclosure of the seriousness of sin, and a sign of Christ's perfect unity with the Father. Thus, they were a necessary and consequential element of the atonement. Campbell, in his further reflections on the perfect confession of Christ as "an equivalent sorrow and repentance," continues and completes the task of demonstrating the necessity of Christ's suffering and death.

Although Campbell was alerted to the possibility of developing an alternate to substituted punishment by a brief allusion of Edwards, it should not be construed by interpreters of Campbell that his attention to Edwards' "an equivalent sorrow and repentance" implies a doctrine of substitutionary repentance similar or parallel to substitutionary punishment. Edwards himself seemed to present the two ideas as parallel concepts but Campbell's development of "equivalent repentance" reveals the two concepts are not parallel. He did not develop Edwards' option of an "equivalent repentance" as a concept intended to replace neatly penal substitution and to leave the basic structure of the doctrine of the atonement unchanged. On the contrary, Campbell's development of Edwards' idea dramatically altered the contours of the doctrine of the atonement as commonly accepted in the Calvinist tradition.

It is precisely here that the origin of confusion, misunderstanding and reductionist readings of Campbell's doctrine can be traced. The assumption that Campbell is setting up an atonement option that parallels penal substitution and only replaces repentance for punishment in the atonement "mechanism" is widely assumed but completely misleading.

The basic distinction between Campbell's discovery of Edwards' idea and how Campbell then actually employed that idea is a crucial one in approaching Campbell's doctrine of the confession of Christ. Again, "repentance" does not merely slide in the place of "punishment" in Campbell's rendering of Christ making a perfect confession or repentance for human sin. The first concept, penal substitution, might be called a "mechanistic image." This doctrine as traditionally expounded states that Christ took on the punishment of God instead of human sinners. The image is one of displacement and replacement, a transaction, a pact - all mechanistic images. The concept Campbell attempted to develop might be called an "organic image." He collected the original idea and terminology from Edwards, but then quickly left behind both Edwards' terminology as well as any hint that the two concepts as stated by Edwards were simply options from the same type of paradigm. Rather, the image of Christ giving a "perfect Amen" to God's judgement of sin is one of inclusion and incorporation, not replacement. In Christ's perfect response, humanity is not replaced; rather, humanity is involved in the sense that Christ makes our own response to God possible.[39]

It is certainly true to say that Campbell intended his concept of Christ making a perfect confession to replace the traditional Calvinist view of penal substitution. But the replacement of Christ-as-Confessor for Christ-as-Punished recasts the picture of what the atonement is, why is was necessary, and what it accomplished. The atonement is not, for Campbell, the means to placate God's wrath so that humanity can be forgiven. Rather, the atonement is the means for God's love to be fully expressed in the life, sufferings, death, and resurrection of Jesus Christ. The atonement is not necessary, for Campbell, so that the fate of humanity for wholesale destruction can be averted through Christ's death and so that God's demands for justice be met. Rather, the atonement is necessary both for a full and complete revelation of God and a full and complete inclusion of humanity as adopted children into God's love. The atonement did not deal with the sins of the elect for the salvation of the elect. Rather, for Campbell, the atonement had a prospective purpose and accomplishment, namely, guaranteeing eternal life in the future and fellowship for the redeemed community in the present.

Misunderstandings concerning Campbell's doctrine of "equivalent repentance" surfaced almost immediately after the publication of Campbell's book. An early reviewer asked, "Is vicarious contrition at all more conceivable than vicarious retribution?"[40] Although Campbell took pains in the second edition of *The Nature of the Atonement* to answer such criticism,[41] it has been a recurring feature of Campbell interpretation that Campbell's concept of Christ's confession is assumed to mean "vicarious confession" or "vicarious repentance."[42] Although these terms are commonly used to designate Campbell's theory, they do not appear in Campbell's own writing.[43]

Some interpreters have attempted to correct the assumption that the concept of Christ's confession simply replaces penal substitution, however Campbell himself may have invited such assumptions by his use of Edwards' brief remark. Brian Gerrish notes that perhaps Campbell fell into a "conceptual indiscretion" in employing Edwards' terminology.[44] Eugene Bewkes agrees. He says, "The reference to Jonathan Edwards' 'equivalent repentance,' for example, has done more to confuse readers than any other thing."[45] Gerrish adds, "The evidence is plain that Campbell did not intend anything so odd as a substitutionary repentance (or a substitutionary anything else), but rather an activity on our behalf into which we are ourselves irresistibly drawn by its sheer moral and spiritual power."[46] George Tuttle, as well, advances the idea that Christ's repentance cannot be conceived as substitutionary in the traditional sense of the term. "The idea of penal substitution means that Christ relieved others of the punishment which was their due by taking it on himself. The idea of Christ's representative repentance, on the other hand, is conceived to be exercised entirely with the prospective purpose that they shall themselves be brought to repentance."[47] It can be concluded that what Campbell perhaps gained in invoking the illustrious name of Edwards he may have lost in the persistent puzzlement surrounding his most central atonement concept.

The terms "vicarious confession" or "vicarious repentance," although not used by Campbell himself, can be usefully employed in a description of Campbell's own atonement theology in a representative sense rather than a substitutionary sense. Provided one understands that the vicarious aspect of Christ's confession is that Christ confessed **on our behalf so that we too can confess**, the term is legitimate. Because subsequent theologians, such as R.C. Moberly, have explicitly taken up the concept of vicarious repentance and others, such as Emil Brunner, have implicitly employed this concept, it is important that the term be very carefully defined in each individual context.[48] Campbell himself, as stated above, did not use the terms "vicarious confession" or "vicarious repentance." He used a variety of phrases in an attempt to get at the core of this atoning work of Christ, including "perfect response," "perfect repentance," "perfect sorrow," "perfect contrition," even "expiatory confession." What this "perfect repentance" accomplishes and how it effects reconciliation is the heart of the issue Campbell attempts to address. He says,

> He who so responds to the divine wrath against sin, saying, "Thou art righteous, O Lord, who judgest so," is necessarily receiving the full apprehension and realisation of that wrath, as well as of that sin against which it comes forth into His soul and spirit, into the bosom of the divine humanity, and, so receiving it, He responds to it with

a perfect response, - a response from the depths of that divine humanity, - and **in that perfect response He absorbs it.** For that response has all the elements of a perfect repentance in humanity for all the sin of man, - a perfect sorrow - a perfect contrition - all the elements of such a repentance, and that in absolute perfection, all - excepting the personal consciousness of sin; - and by that perfect response in Amen to the mind of God in relation to sin is the wrath of God rightly met, and that is accorded to divine justice which is its due, and could alone satisfy it.[49]

This densely packed section contains the key features of Campbell's concept of Christ-as-Confessor. Because Christ, in his "divine humanity" fully realized the sorrow and wrath of God against sin and fully acknowledged and confessed the justice and righteousness of that sorrow and wrath, Christ was able to make a perfect and complete response both to the horror of sin and the holiness of God. That response can only be called a "perfect contrition" or a "perfect sorrow." Its effect was to "absorb" the wrath of God and so atone for the sin of humanity and bring reconciliation between God and humanity.

What does it actually mean that Christ's repentance or contrition or sorrow "absorbed" the wrath of God? Beyond this crucial and ambiguous word of explication, Campbell does not and cannot go much farther. It is the very core of the atonement mystery in Campbell's theology. Every atonement theory has its central mystery - the place where, finally, explanations of how God reconciled the world to Godself in the life and death of Jesus Christ end.[50] For Campbell, the central mystery is the absorption of God's wrath in Christ's own perfect response to God's just judgement and his realization of sin in his own spirit. In this, somehow, is salvation. In this, somehow, God's justice is satisfied and human need is met.

It must be admitted that Campbell's brief and cryptic mention of the "absorption" of God's wrath by Christ's confession is an attempt to explicate what is more completely accounted for in some of the atonement theologies he rejected. For it is precisely here that the notion of penal substitution makes its most persuasive case. Whatever difficult attendant problems penal substitution has for an overall atonement account, it does explain the sufferings and death of Christ as something utterly necessary for our salvation, completely effective in breaking the power of sin, and congruent to a God of law and justice.

Campbell rejected penal substitution because it had been formulated by scholastic and covenantal theologians as a device to appease the wrath of God. From this concept, Campbell rightly recoiled. But if the notion of penal substitution could be articulated in a way that would clearly place it under the broader framework of the love of God, perhaps Campbell would have, at least in some modified way, retained it. It is this approach to the doctrine of penal substitution that Karl Barth attempted in his section on "The Judge Judged in Our Place" in IV/1 of the *Church Dogmatics*. Instead of the mercy and justice of God existing in uneasy confrontation, Barth sees both the mercy and justice of God embraced by the larger category of God's love. Campbell would have heartily agreed. His primary motivation to reject penal substitution was to advance the love of God as God's foundational attribute. Campbell did not, however, consider a possible reformulation of penal substitution in order to assure this foundational axiom.

Further exploration of Barth's complex atonement theology is not possible here, but it is interesting to note that Barth and Campbell shared a similar theological motive, that is, to highlight and make central the love of God. However, that shared motive issued in very different atonement accounts, Campbell rejecting and Barth maintaining the notion of penal substitution, although in a secondary and carefully controlled role.

Campbell used new, unfamiliar terminology to attempt to account for the inner workings of God's salvation in Jesus Christ. Christ-as-Confessor does not mean that Christ took on a personal consciousness of sin and the weight of guilt and then repented **instead** of us, in a substitutionary sense. Rather, Christ acknowledged fully and perfectly the scandal of sin and the righteousness of God and **in that response**, sin is conquered, God is satisfied, and we are thus called to be partakers through Christ in eternal life.[51] This is the whole point:

that Christ's perfect response was accomplished **on our behalf** so that we are ourselves irresistibly drawn by its sheer moral and spiritual power to repentance and a full realization of our status as adopted children of God.

Vincent Taylor is convinced Campbell caught the right sense of Christ's representative sacrificial work in his concept of perfect confession. He says, in reference to Campbell, "We need a category of representative action, which describes a work of Christ for men so altogether great and inclusive that they cannot accomplish it for themselves, but which, far from being external to themselves, and therefore substitutionary, is a vital factor in their approach to God, because in it they can participate both by personal faith and in corporate worship."[52]

Critical evaluation of Campbell's entire atonement theology usually focuses on this crucial idea of Christ's confession. Theologians and believers who are committed to or accustomed to the more traditional doctrine of penal substitution may find Campbell's account curiously "soft" or "undramatic." It seems to them less stirring and climactic than the doctrine that Christ suffered all the wrath of God instead of us and thus set us free from the threat of the punishment properly due us. Campbell's language of "spiritual and moral" power strikes others as merely subjective and individualistic. An additional objection is that Campbell's theory seems to receive scant support from Scripture. There are a number of hurdles in considering Campbell's theory as a serious contender for a valid atonement theology.

Campbell was fully aware of these objections to his atonement theology and tried to meet some of them in his book, especially in an appendix to the second edition as well as in letters to family and friends. With respect to the objection that Scriptural support is dubious for the concept of vicarious confession, he remarks that he wishes he could take the time and space in his book to look at all the Scriptures commonly taken to show the doctrine of penal substitution and demonstrate how they have much more to say of a moral and spiritual atonement.[53]

With respect to the charge that this concept misses the power and drama of the penal substitution view, Campbell most emphatically disagrees. He denies that his theology ignores the horror and scandal of sin and insists that the believer must know "the deep and awful impression of what sin must be in the eyes of God . . ."[54] It would be a momentous theological mistake to softpedal or mute the harsh legacy of sin. Furthermore, Campbell is convinced that the drama of Christ making a full, complete, and perfect response to the holy judgement of God and meeting that judgement in his own spirit, contains far more power and drama and truth than all the pains of penal substitution.[55]

As far as the objection that Campbell's theology here tilts dangerously toward subjectivism and individualism, nothing could be farther from his intent. A main theme in Campbell's atonement theology is to emphasize quite the opposite. Believers can be confident in their salvation because they are **not** required individually to examine evidences of their election.[56] Rather, the whole purpose of Christ's salvific work is to bring humanity into the new redeemed community of God's adopted children. The community of believers can be utterly confident in their knowledge and faith of God's unfailing love and mercy. Campbell's theology is decidedly community-oriented and Kingdom-focused.

It is clear in the *Memorials* that common objections to his atonement account occupied Campbell's mind for many years and he continually tried to clarify and specify his thoughts. In a letter recorded in *Memorials*, Principal Shairp, a friend of Campbell, recalled how Campbell tried to explain the necessity of Christ's suffering and death for our salvation. He remembered that Campbell said that salvation "can only enter into in and through the shedding of the blood of Jesus. 'The wages of sin is death.' This is the Father's eternal irreversible way of looking at sin. He does not change this will. But Christ meets this will, says, 'Thou art righteous, O Father, in thus judging sin; and I accept Thy judgment of it; and meet it. I in my humanity say Amen to Thy judgment of sin.' "[57]

Here it is clear that Campbell did not espouse a mere "moral and spiritual" atonement. Much of Campbell's language, especially in the

118

Memorials account above, is very similar to the traditional language of the Reformed tradition of which Campbell was an heir. Something objective happened, something located in the time and space of Jesus of Nazareth's life on earth. What precisely that "something" is seems to be beyond the reach of human language and human comprehension. The best Campbell can say is that Christ both gave the perfect response to God's wrath against sin and felt that wrath in his own spirit, thus meeting the holiness and justice of God and drawing humanity into a new redeemed community. Because of the life, suffering, death, and resurrection of Jesus Christ, sin is defeated, God is honored, and humanity is called to new life.

The Relationship of Christ to Human Persons

The question of how human persons get connected to the saving work of Christ is a central issue in Christology and soteriology. It is a question of the relationship of Christ to human persons. This foundational issue has been answered variously in the history of Christian reflection. Some theological images available in atonement theology are inclusion, participation, divinization, imputation, union with Christ through the Spirit, and adoption.

Another image in the history of Christian reflection on the connection between Christ and the human believer is suggested by Kenneth Surin in his focus on the theological doctrine of the *imago Dei*. On this view, Christ is meaningfully and personally connected to human persons because humanity is created in the image of God. Surin says, "Through the *imago Dei*, then, we have a means of expressing the principle that God is, to some degree, and in a suitably qualified sense, present in all his creatures."[58] Surin admits that the *imago Dei* does not explicitly account for how it is that **Christ** is savingly connected to human persons. He suggests linking the image of God concept with a recapitulation theory similar to that of Irenaeus to conceive of how Jesus Christ can and did re-create a new humanity and thus involve and include all human persons. The possibility of a connection between humanity and Christ is established by the *imago Dei* because Christ is both human and divine, both the source of the *imago Dei* as well as its first and decisive recipient. The connection becomes actual with Christ reversing the cycle of sin's destruction and establishing a re-created humanity.

Another option on stating the relationship between Christ and human persons arises in reflecting on one interpreter's reading of Athanasius' treatise, *On the Incarnation*. It is the belief of George Dion Dragas that Athanasius must not be read as holding either a straight-forward Platonic realism or a simple forensic sacrifice theory.[59] Rather, Christ is connected to, and represents, humanity by virtue of the fact that Christ is the Logos of creation. Athanasius, on Dragas' account, uses realist categories but his realism posits an individual human nature in Christ which then, because it subsists in the Creator/Logos, can and does have genuine connection to other individual persons. Dragas explains, "Thus the inner logic, as it were, of this substitutionary act is not to be traced to an abstract principle of forensic sacrificial transaction but to the headship of the Divine Logos in creation whereby he is related to all human beings and as such can act on their behalf as their true representative."[60] Dragas means by this that Christ's sacrifice is efficacious because Christ is the Head of all creation. The connection is established through Christ as source and origin of all humanity.

Another attempt to explicate the relationship between Christ and the believer is made by James B. Torrance, Thomas F. Torrance, and several others in the concept of the "vicarious humanity of Christ." These theologians believe "vicarious humanity" is the best designation of Campbell's view of Christ's connection to human persons.[61] They are convinced that the humanity of Christ provides a basis for the knowledge of God, a foundation for reconciliation between God and humanity, and an account of humanity's participation in salvation. Through Christ's humanity, God has made a commitment to all humanity and has, in fact, brought humanity into the life of God.[62]

The term "vicarious humanity" is extraordinarily evocative and rich but its meaning is not immediately clear and transparent. In what sense is Christ's humanity **vicarious**? T.F. Torrance apparently intends to say by this term that all humanity participates in the benefits of the salvific work of Christ by virtue of Christ's true humanity. He says, for instance that the humanity of Christ is "the **arche** of the new humanity. As the incarnate Son of God he became one body with us in order to gather up our corrupt humanity into bodily existence in himself, healing and renewing it within himself through the perfection and holiness of his own human nature and life.. . . It is that consecrated humanity in Jesus Christ which constitutes the life-giving substance of the Church and the perpetual source of its renewal."[63] In other words, according to T.F. Torrance, Christ "lays hold of us in himself and acts for us from out of the inner depths of his coexistence with us and our existence in him. . ."[64]   Thus, humanity vicariously participates in Christ's humanity as Christ vicariously participates in all humanity by virtue of his inclusive and consummating incarnation.   The vicarious relationship is a dynamic one which applies both from human persons to Christ and Christ to human persons.[65]   Another Campbell interpreter follows Torrance in saying that, "Christ's participation in our life constitutes the way in which we may participate in his life and thus be what we are meant to be under God."[66]

Perhaps the most comprehensive definition of the term is that of J.B. Torrance,

> Such is the wonderful love of God that He has come to us, not simply in a man but **as man** in Jesus Christ, assumed our life, underwritten our responsibilities, offered for us once and for all a life of worship and obedience and prayer to the Father, taken to Himself our unworthy body of death, vicariously submitted for us to the verdict of guilty, died our death, risen again in our humanity, returned to the Father as our Advocate and Memorial in the presence of God, so that **by grace** his life is our life, His death our death, His victory our victory, His resurrection our resurrection, His righteousness our righteousness, and His eternal prayers and self-offering to the Father our prayers and offering in the presence of the Father.[67]

Although "vicarious humanity" is clearly a term intended to be wide-ranging and evocative, it may be too rich, too dense. Indeed,

Kettler lists nine theses which attempt to unpack the content of this laden expression.[68] The term "vicarious humanity" is so multi-faceted and complex that it soon becomes clear it is a term which attempts to embrace the full reality of the Incarnation and the implications of the Incarnation for human redemption. In order to explicate carefully Campbell's view of the relationship between Christ and the believer, a formulation with a sharper cutting edge and more precision may be helpful.

The importance of this issue of Christ's bond with the believer was highlighted in an early review of Campbell's book. There, the reviewer, James Martineau, accused Campbell of "individualism," by which he means the theory of "the inalienable and separate character of all particular persons, taken one by one. . ." which precludes the possibility of a mediation between God and humanity by Christ.[69] In other words, the reviewer complained that Campbell's view of the human person and of Christ is highly individualist, such that there is no path of mediation or interaction by Christ between human persons and God.

In the face of this charge, Campbell was understandably per-plexed. He said,

"In reading the latter part of his review, I have felt that the 'individualism' and the 'realism' of which he speaks have been to me a Scylla and a Charybdis, between which I have steered in the dark, unconsciously, while I trust safely. I have had no conception of an 'individualism' which made my personality so cut me off from Christ that I could not, except by a moral or legal fiction, represent Him to myself as under the pressure of my sins, both confessing them before the Father, and pleading with the Father on my behalf. I had no conception of a 'realism' which represented humanity as one whole in such a sense as would have lost to me my personality, or would have helped me to the faith of an atonement by justifying me in looking upon Christ, as 'realism' appears to the reviewer to have led Luther to do, as *literally* 'the one sinner,' chargeable, therefore, with all the sins of all partakers in humanity."[70]

Campbell exhibits a grasp of what is at stake here. He realizes that "individualism" implies that all human persons are so distinct and autonomous that the person and work of Christ can only be applied to them by a "moral or legal fiction," for example, an imputation of Christ's benefits or declaration of a new legal standing. He realizes as well that "realism" implies an ontological level of reality that merges or fuses all discreet human persons into one principal of Humanity or conceives of all human persons as partakers of the One Person, Jesus Christ. Campbell seems to say by his remark of steering between the Scylla and Charybdis that he is neither an "individualist" or a "realist." In effect, he is saying, "If those are the only two choices, I hold neither." He is uncomfortable with the two choices, the one which conceives of the human individual as solitary, unconnected, and autonomous and the other which conceives of all human persons as individuations of one consummating principle.

Campbell believes the choice between "realism" and "individualism" posited by Martineau is a false choice. Rather, he assumes both "the relation of Christ to humanity along with a recognition of our personal individuality."[71] Campbell does not, though, in response to his critical reviewer, articulate the philosophical and theological contours of that relationship which he says he assumes. In fact, he believes that the relationship between Christ and humanity is one of the central mysteries of the atonement. Near the end of the book, in the context of justifying the project of the book, he admits his own limitations in understanding the atonement. For him, the chief mystery is not grasping the efficacy of the salvific work of Christ. Rather, the chief mystery is the nature of the relationship between Christ and humanity. He says,

"But the nature of the relation of the Son of God to humanity, whether we contemplate His own personal work in making His soul an offering for sin, making an end of sin, and bringing in everlasting righteousness, or His work in men as putting forth the power in them which is implied in His being their life; - this belongs to the acting of God, as God, and to the divinity of the Son of God, in an

aspect of the subject which all experience in thinking of our relation
to God prepares us to find ourselves unable to understand."[72]

Campbell indicates by this statement that to answer the question,
"How is Christ 'in us' and how are we 'in Christ'?" is to exceed the
limits of theological inquiry and articulation.[73] He makes only a
brief suggestion, but offers no further exposition. The suggestion,
contained in the above quote, is that this relationship between Christ
and the believer, finds its source in the "acting of God" and the
"divinity of the Son of God." Beyond this statement of faith,
Campbell does not venture further.[74] But it must not be concluded
that he pleads an easy agnosticism with respect to difficult theological
problems. He admits the limits of rational reflection only reluctantly,
but then, with gratitude for what that mystery reveals. Although we
cannot specify the nature of the relation between Christ and the
Christian, Campbell said, we can know, experience, and live in the
benefits which that relationship guarantees us.[75]

Campbell does not, in *The Nature of the Atonement* or anywhere
else, suggest a precise and conceptually rigorous account of the
relationship between Christ and human persons or other issues in
Christology. He does not, for instance, attempt to specify the nature
of Christ's person, how Christ is human and divine, the coherence of
Chalcedon, or his theological affinities to either an Alexandrian or an
Antiochan form of Christological expression. The interpreter of
Campbell has only to rely on the evidence of the text and what can
reasonably or plausibly be deduced from the rather peculiar and
idiosyncratic Christological expressions Campbell uses.

Some of these characteristic Christological expressions have come
to light in the context of explicating Campbell's atonement theology.
Expressions such as "the divine mind in Christ," "oneness of mind
with the Father," "meeting the divine mind," "divine love in humanity," "response of the mind of the Son to the mind of the Father,"
"sonship in humanity," "divine transaction in humanity," are all
phrases Campbell employs to reveal his notion of the intimate union
of Christ with his Father in love as well as the intimate union of
Christ with humanity in love. Campbell does not typically use the

language of "human nature" and "divine nature," preferring instead terms that emphasize the relationship of sonship to the Father and brotherhood to humanity. It is a unproductive exercise to scrutinize Campbell's terminology for precise Christological declarations. To attempt, for example, to analyze the phrase "sonship in humanity" for possible traces of Nestorianism or Adoptionism, or, for that matter, for a possible expression of Chalcedonian orthodoxy, is to subject Campbell's terminology to a test it had no intention of meeting in the first place. The genuinely puzzling array of Campbell's terminology must be seen as his creative effort to express the core of the relationship between the Son and the Father and the Son and human believers.

There is no hint by these characteristic expressions that Campbell muted either the full divinity of Christ or the full humanity of Christ. In fact, his theology of the sufferings of Christ fully insures the complete human experience of Jesus Christ, excepting sin. His consistent emphasis on the Incarnation as the presupposition of the atonement and on Christ's intimate communion with the Father fully insures the complete divinity of Jesus Christ.[76]

It is not surprising to discover that Campbell's language about the person of Christ is in close accord with the basic presuppositions of his theology. Because Campbell's primary motivation in his reflections on the atonement is to highlight the love and mercy of God, he repeatedly makes a connection between the earthly life of Jesus Christ and how that life displays and embodies the love of the Father. For example, Christ on earth was "living the life of love in humanity" or he is the "love that came into humanity."[77]

Love is not only displayed by the Incarnation but it is the actualizing power of the Incarnation. Campbell has no interest in speculating how it is that Jesus Christ **can** be both fully divine and fully human. Instead, he starts with the fact, accepted by faith, of the Incarnation and inquires **how** Incarnation develops naturally to atonement and, still naturally, leads further to the participation of human believers in the divine life.[78] "Thus **related to us**, while **by love identified with us**, the son of God necessarily came under all our burdens. . .," says Campbell, and in that brief statement the mystery of Christ's relationship to human persons is revealed.[79]

Again, Campbell has no interest in pursuing the ontological implications of a realist or a nominalist reading of Christ's connection with human persons. For him, the whole point of inquiring into the relationship between Christ and humanity is to make explicit that the relationship of love and trust Christ had with the Father is the same relationship of love and trust individual human persons can now have, on account of Christ, with God.[80] Through Christ's perfect response to the holiness of God and his complete acknowledgement of the sorrow sin has brought to the Father's heart, Christ brings us into the same relationship with the Father that he so unwaveringly experienced.[81] How we are related to Christ, how we are "in Christ," how Christ's salvific work is connected to us, is all by virtue of the fact that Christ, identified with us by love, inaugurates and incorporates us into the new redeemed community.

So, Campbell can say with St. Paul, "I am crucified with Christ; nevertheless I live; yet not I, but Christ liveth in me, and the life which I now live in the flesh I live by the faith of the Son of God, who loved me, and gave Himself for me."[82] As far as whether this conception of being united with Christ in love can withstand the scrutiny of metaphysical thought, Campbell candidly admits that, "neither can metaphysical thought reveal to us the manner of our own being as God's offspring, who live and move and have our being in Him, or **the relations to us into which the Eternal Son has come that He might be in us the life of Sonship.**"[83]

Thus, it can be seen that Campbell's view of the relationship between Christ and the believer, like his entire theology, has a decidedly **prospective** direction. Christ's "divine sonship in humanity" must be replicated and reproduced in the community in a full awareness by believers of their own status as adopted sons and daughters. In fact, Campbell says that unless the work of redemption is duplicated in humanity, its full excellence cannot be realized.[84] He insists that "faith in Christ **as my life** as well as faith in Christ as having died for me" are both necessary for a full understanding of Christ's work.[85]

This section has demonstrated Campbell's strong sense that our connection to Christ is through a bond of love that is displayed and actualized in the life of the believing community. The basis of this relationship is the desire of divine love which is made concrete by God in Christ. The relationship is actualized by the bond of love Christ has to the believing community through the activity of the Holy Spirit.[86] The relationship demonstrates its reality and vitality when this bond of love is expanded and extended into the life of the community identified by its vibrant assurance of adoption into God's love.

NOTES

1. A.B. Macaulay, in *The Death of Jesus* (London: Hodder and Stoughton, 1938), p. 141ff, said that Campbell's treatment of the cry of dereliction is docetic. R.C. Moberly objects to Campbell's view of the cry of dereliction as well: ". . . it is impossible not to feel that he has not so much explained the cry, as explained it away." *Atonement and Personality* (New York: Longmans, Green, and Co., 1901), p. 407. Further discussion of Campbell's approach to the cry of dereliction will appear below.

2. R.S. Paul, *The Atonement and the Sacraments* (Nashville: Abingdon Press, 1960), p.146; George Carey, *The Gate of Glory*, p. 130; John R.W. Stott, *The Cross of Christ*, pp. 141-143. It should be noted that none of these critiques are carefully worked out. Interpreters of Campbell who criticize his theory of the sufferings of Christ usually approach the subject assuming that the penal substitution theory is the only acceptable explanation of Christ's sufferings.

3. *The Nature of the Atonement*, p. 51.

4. Campbell was an admirer and close reader of Edwards and a friend and colleague of Chalmers. That he was not aware of their differences both in theology and context is hardly possible. Although his references to Owen occur only in chapter three in *The Nature of the Atonement*, his knowledge of Owen was most likely fairly complete, since Owen was, and is, a standard of orthodox Calvinist theology.

5. Amy Plantinga Pauw, in her 1990 Yale University dissertation, *"The Supreme Harmony of All:" Jonathan Edwards and the Trinity*, convincingly demonstrates the distinct position of Edwards on the atonement from that of either his Puritan and scholastic forebears and his Edwardsean, federalist successors. Plantinga Pauw traces Edwards' debts to his predecessors and his contributions to the following generation of theologians, but claims that with respect to the atonement the differences between Edwards and his predecessors as well as the Edwardseans are more prominent than the resemblances.

6. Ralph Wardlaw (1779-1853) was a Scottish congregationalist divine who served an independent church in Glasgow until his death. Wardlaw was a well-known preacher in Scotland, England, and America and so it is not surprising that Campbell knew of him and his theological writings. It is also quite likely that Campbell knew him personally, since they both served independent congregations in Glasgow for many years. Wardlaw's book on the atonement, *Discourses on the Nature and Extent of the Atonement of Christ* (Glasgow: James Maclehose, 1844) enjoyed the success of two editions.

George Payne (1781-1848) was a British congregationalist divine who did his theological training at Glasgow.

John Pye Smith (1774-1851) was also British. He was a sort of Renaissance man, lecturing in the humanities, Hebrew, Greek, logic, rhetoric, mathematics and science, and theology. *The Dictionary of National Biography*, ed. Leslie Stephen and Sidney Lee, vol. xvii (Oxford: Oxford University Press, 1973), p. 494, called Pye Smith's treatise on the atonement a "minor work," yet Campbell chose to use Pye Smith as one of his proponents of federal theology. This "minor work," nonetheless, *Four Discourses on the Sacrifice and Priesthood of Jesus Christ and the Atonement and Redemption Thence Accruing*, 4th ed. (Edinburgh: William Oliphant and Co.), 1859), was reissued four times.

Thomas W. Jenkyn wrote a well-received book on the atonement in 1846 which enjoyed several British and American editions, was a student and friend of John Pye Smith, and served as president of Coward College in London. His book, *The Extent of the Atonement in its Relation to God and the Universe* (Boston: Gould, Kendall and Lincoln), is noted for its rejection of a limited atonement as well as its strongly federal framework.

Why Campbell did not choose more prominent federal or covenant theologians is puzzling. Scottish theologians such as Samuel Rutherford, David Dickson, and James Durham are much better known as representative federalists. Perhaps Campbell wanted to employ the work of people contemporary with him or, perhaps, he knew personally all three of these people. There is no evidence for this in any of his correspondence, however.

7. John Pye Smith, *Four Discourses*, p. 4.

8. *The Nature of the Atonement*, p. 83.

9. The phrase "axiomatic defect" is on p. 54 of *The Nature of the Atonement*.

10. *The Nature of the Atonement*, p. 115. Emphasis mine.

11. *The Nature of the Atonement*, p. 117.

12. Campbell quotes Edwards in support of that part of his argument which proposes that the sufferings of Christ were not punishment but were the form of holiness and love under pressure from sin. Although Campbell quotes Edwards at some length, he, typically, does not cite the source.

It appears, in the passage Campbell selected, that Edwards' meaning in the citation is not exactly what Campbell proposes. Edwards suggests that it is God who lays the suffering of Christ on him; the connection does not seem **natural**, as Campbell wishes to insist. Part of the unidentified Edwards' citation is: ". . . Christ loving the elect with a perfect love, God was able - by bearing in upon Christ's spirit the perfect realisation of what these objects of His love were exposed to suffer - to make, through His love to them, their conceived-of suffering, real, infinite suffering to Him."

Thus, Edwards supports Campbell in that Christ's sufferings were not equivalent to human sin, but he does not appear to support Campbell's additional claim that the sufferings must have a natural connection to Christ's love and holiness.

13. *The Nature of the Atonement*, p. 130.

14. *The Nature of the Atonement*, p. 130.

15. *The Nature of the Atonement*, p. 133.

16. *The Nature of the Atonement*, p. 134.

17. *The Nature of the Atonement*, p. 275.

18. *The Nature of the Atonement*, p. 280.

19. *The Nature of the Atonement*, p. 281, 282.

20. Campbell says, ". . . that fatherliness in God, in which the Sinless One is trusting, is a fatherliness in which the sinful may trust" (p. 309).

21. I owe these reflections to Tuttle, *So Rich a Soil*, p. 124, 125.

22. Campbell uses the language of the wrath of God only very infrequently. In his efforts to highlight and emphasize the love and mercy of God, he seems reluctant to discuss God's wrath at all. But here he says, ". . . we feel that here we have come to that which men have contemplated when they have conceived of Christ as satisfying divine justice in respect of its claim for vengeance upon our sins." *The Nature of the Atonement*, p. 134.

23. *The Nature of the Atonement*, p. 134.

24. Although, it must be admitted, Campbell uses this terminology only very infrequently.

25. This important concept will be developed in chapter five, namely, how Campbell's concept of satisfaction operates in his atonement theology.

26. *The Nature of the Atonement*, p. 136. Emphasis Campbell's. An analysis of this critical concept in Campbell's atonement theology will be undertaken later in this chapter. Here the focus is on the sufferings of Christ.

27. *The Nature of the Atonement*, p. 293.

28. *The Nature of the Atonement*, p. 140.

29. *The Nature of the Atonement*, p. 287. Also p. 290 where Campbell says, ". . . though God's wrath against sin was not felt by the Son of God as coming forth against Himself personally, as if the Father saw Him as a sinner; yet must that wrath in the truth of what it is have been present to and realised by His spirit; - and though He suffered not from it as having its revenges inflicted on Him, yet must the realisation of it and confession of its righteousness, in perfect sympathy with that righteousness, have been a suffering proportioned to His spiritual perfection; and while He interceded in the faith of the infinite love of the Father and knowing that the will of God was our salvation, yet must the love that was taking this form have suffered in itself, while interceding, all the pain proper to the heart of perfect sonship, in its sympathy with the feelings of perfect fatherhood against which His brethren had sinned."

30. Campbell's emphasis on the humanity of Christ in this direction can be discerned in statements like, "This witness-bearing for God . . . was accomplished in the personal perfection that was in Christ, His manifested

perfection in humanity . . . and the perfection of His brotherly love in His walk with men." *The Nature of the Atonement*, p. 129.

31. Campbell rarely uses the traditional terms "divine and human natures". He is fond of terms like "divinity in humanity" or "divine humanity" or "mind of the Father" or "mind of the Son."

32. *The Nature of the Atonement*, Chapters 11 and 12.

33. *The Nature of the Atonement*, p. 288. Emphasis mine.

34. *The Nature of the Atonement*, pp. 258-261.

35. *The Nature of the Atonement*, p. 260, 295. A strength of Campbell's theology, as was noted in chapter two, is his continual effort to relate Christ's salvific work with the life of the believing community. Put in Campbell's own terms, this is an example of how the retrospective and the prospective aspects of the atonement form a unity.

36. *The Nature of the Atonement*, p. 262, 292.

37. *The Nature of the Atonement*, pp. 135, 136, emphasis Campbell's.

38. Jonathan Edwards, 'Satisfaction for Sin', in *The Works of President Edwards* (New York, 1844), ii, 1-3.

39. This concept of inclusion and incorporation will be considered later in this chapter in the final section on Christ's relationship to humanity.

40. James Martineau, "Mediatorial Religion", *Studies of Christianity; Timely Thoughts for Religious Thinkers*, ed. W.R. Alger (Boston: American Unitarian Association, 1875), p. 168. Martineau's review was first published in the April, 1856, *National Review* but is reprinted in the cited volume.

41. *The Nature of the Atonement*, pp. 398-401.

42. A.B. Bruce, in *The Humiliation of Christ* 2nd ed. (New York: A.C. Armstrong & Son, 1887), is another example of the mistaken assumption of a parallel relationship between the two concepts of substituted punishment and substituted repentance. He says, "The theory has been treated by critics of all schools as the eccentricity of a devout author, who, dissatisfied with the traditional theory, has substituted in its place another, involving not only greater difficulty, but even something very like absurdity" (p. 320). J.K.

Mozley also assumes Campbell's view of vicarious repentance substitutes for vicarious punishment in *The Doctrine of the Atonement* (New York: Charles Scribner's Sons, 1916), p. 193, as does G.B. Stevens in *Christian Doctrine of Salvation* (New York: Charles Scribner's Son, 1905), p. 213. Vincent Taylor, in "The Best Books on the Atonement," *The Expository Times* 48 (Oct. 1936-Sep. 1937), p. 269, displays this assumption as well, "As is well known, Campbell substitutes for the theory of vicarious punishment the thought of a vicarious repentance which Christ as the representative and complete man was able to offer for men." But Eugene Bewkes rightly claims that Campbell's theory "has been mistakenly classified as substitutionary repentance." Cf. *Legacy of a Christian Mind*, p. 182.

43. "Vicarious repentance" appears in the title of an article on Campbell by Christian D. Kettler, "The Vicarious Repentance of Christ in the Theology of John McLeod Campbell and R.C. Moberly," *Scottish Journal of Theology* 38 (1985), pp. 529-543. James B. Torrance, in "The Contribution of McLeod Campbell to Scottish Theology," in *Scottish Journal of Theology* 26 (1973), p. 306, also calls Campbell's theory "vicarious penitence," although he adds that this has often been misunderstood. H.R. MacIntosh also employs this term, in reference to Campbell, in a chapter entitled, "The Vicarious Repentance of Christ," from *Some Aspects of Christian Belief* (London: Hodder and Stoughton, 1924).

44. Gerrish, *Tradition and the Modern World: Reformed Theology in the Nineteenth Century*, p. 87.

45. Bewkes, *Legacy of a Christian Mind*, p. 186.

46. Gerrish, *Tradition and the Modern World; Reformed Theology in the Nineteenth Century*, p. 208, fn. 52.

47. Tuttle, *So Rich a Soil*, p. 129.

48. R.C. Moberly explicitly traces his doctrine of Christ repenting for humanity's sin to McLeod Campbell. On p. 405 in *Atonement and Personality*, he states his own quite different version of the concept, "He [Christ] confessed the sin of humanity by *being* the very manifestation of humanity, in its ideal reality of penitential holiness, before the Father." C.S. Lewis entitled a chapter in *Mere Christianity* (New York: Macmillan, 1958), "The Perfect Penitent." Emil Brunner, in *The Mediator*, trans. Olive Wyon (Philadelphia: Westminster Press, 1947), p. 534, echoes Campbell when he says, "If we could repent as we should no atonement would be needed, for then repentance would be atonement. Then the righteousness of God would

132

have been satisfied. But this is precisely what we cannot do. . . The sacrifice of the Mediator . . . therefore is necessary because only 'in Christ,' and indeed in the Cross of Christ, can we really repent." Brunner knew of John McLeod Campbell and refers to him with warmth in *The Christian Doctrine of Creation and of Redemption; Dogmatics, vol. II*, trans. Olive Wyon (Philadelphia: Westminster Press, 1952), p. 315.

49. *The Nature of the Atonement*, p. 137. Emphasis Campbell's.

50. There are some who have chosen to dismiss Campbell on the basis of his inability to account exactly for the mechanism of this concept of the atonement. But it must be admitted that there are excruciating difficulties in the theory of penal substitution as well. Specifically, those difficulties include how it is that a perfect Christ **can** suffer as a substitute for deserved human punishment, whether Christ bears guilt as well as punishment, how it is that God can be both loving and wrathful, and what the precise nature of Christ's substitution might be.

51. *The Nature of the Atonement*, p. 150. Note how naturally the retrospective aspect of the atonement leads to and is linked to the prospective aspect. Once again, the inherent unity of Campbell's theory can be demonstrated.

52. Vincent Taylor, *The Atonement in New Testament Teaching* (London: Epworth Press, 1954), p. 198.

53. *The Nature of the Atonement*, p. 315.

54. *The Nature of the Atonement*, p. 312. Also *Memorials*, vol. 2, p. 343.

55. Campbell is always somewhat surprised that anyone would find the concept of substituted punishment as more redemptive, more powerful, more divine than Christ's confession-in-humanity before the Father. He remarks, with some puzzlement, that people "more easily believe that Christ's sufferings shew how God can punish sin, than that these sufferings are the divine feelings in relation to sin. . . Yet however the former may terrify, the latter alone can purify. . ." (p. 141). He says later on, "that there would be atoning worth in one tear of the true and perfect sorrow . . . than in endless ages of penal woe" (p. 146).

56. It will be remembered that Campbell's convictions concerning this foundational issue was a primary reason why Campbell attracted the censure of the Church of Scotland in 1831 and was deposed from the ordained ministry.

57. *Memorials*, Vol. 2, p. 343.

58. Kenneth Surin, "Atonement and Christology," *Zeitschrift fur Systematische Theologie* 24 (1955), p. 143, 144.

59. George Dion Dragas, "St. Athanasius on Christ's Sacrifice," *Sacrifice and Redemption; Durham Essays in Theology*, ed. Stephen W. Sykes (Cambridge: Cambridge University Press, 1991), p. 92. This view on Athanasius is held, for instance, by J.N.D. Kelly in *Early Christian Doctrine* (New York: Harper & Row, 1978), p. 378. The various interpretations on Athanasius illustrate that the details of this issue are complex, deserving more careful attention than this brief survey can allow.

60. Dragas, "St. Athanasius on Christ's Sacrifice," p. 93.

61. T.F. Torrance discusses this concept in "The Mind of Christ in Worship: The Problem of Apollinarianism in the Liturgy," *Theology in Reconciliation* (London: Geoffrey Chapman Publishers, 1975), pp. 139-214. James B. Torrance uses this term with reference to Campbell in, "The Contribution of McLeod Campbell to Scottish Theology," *Scottish Journal of Theology* 26 (1973), p. 305 and in "The Vicarious Humanity of Christ," *The Incarnation*, ed. T.F. Torrance (Edinburgh: Handsell Press, 1981), pp. 127-147. Christian Kettler, a student of J.B. Torrance develops this idea as well in *The Vicarious Humanity of Christ and the Reality of Salvation* (New York: University Press of America, 1991), pp. 155-186. Daniel P. Thimell develops the insights of James B. Torrance in his "Christ in Our Place in the Theology of John McLeod Campbell," *Christ in Our Place; The Humanity of God in Christ for the Reconciliation of the World*, ed. Trevor Hart and Daniel Thimell, (Exeter: Paternoster Press, 1989), pp. 182-206.

62. Kettler, *The Vicarious Humanity of Christ and the Reality of Salvation*, p. 136. Kettler wrote a 1987 Fuller Theological Seminary Ph.D. dissertation on John McLeod Campbell, using Torrance's terminology of vicarious humanity as a major interpretive category. This book expands and develops the thesis of his dissertation.

63. Thomas F. Torrance, *The Trinitarian Faith; The Evangelical Theology of the Ancient Catholic Church* (Edinburgh: T & T Clark, 1988), p. 267.

64. Torrance, *The Trinitarian Faith*, p. 155.

65. T.F. Torrance suggests that early theologians such as Athanasius used a profusion of prepositional expressions precisely in an effort to capture this sense of the vicarious humanity of Christ and the vicarious humanity of human persons. Such prepositional expressions include "for us," "for our sake," "for our salvation," "on our behalf," "in our place," "in our stead," "for our need." *The Trinitarian Faith*, p. 168.

66. Tuttle, *So Rich a Soil*, p. 134.

67. J.B. Torrance, "The Vicarious Humanity and Priesthood of Christ in the Theology of John Calvin," *Calvinus Ecclesiae Doctor; Die Referate des Congrès International de Recherches Calviniennes vom 25 bis 28 September, 1978 in Amsterdam*, ed. W.H. Neuser (Kampen: J.H. Kok B.V., 1978), p. 71.

68. Kettler, *The Vicarious Humanity of Christ and the Reality of Salvation* (Lanham, Maryland: University Press of America, 1991), p. 127, 128.

69. James Martineau, "Mediatorial Religion," p. 171. Martineau was a prominent and prolific British Unitarian of the nineteenth century. His review is characterized by a curious combination of perceptive and astute assessment as well as sarcasm and sharp criticism. In addition, it makes several glaring errors, such as the claim that the sufferings and death of Christ go unexplained in Campbell's atonement theology. Martineau also used this review to expound Unitarian teaching by attempting to debunk the orthodox doctrine of the Trinity.

The first two sentences of the review read, "This is a strange book. A Greek would have hated it" (p. 147). He continues with a sarcastic appraisal of Campbell's style, "Cumbrous, tiresome, monotonous, it has few attractions for the natural man, who may have a weakness in favor of pure English and nice grammar" (p. 147). Campbell, in his reply to Martineau in an appendix to the second edition of *The Nature of the Atonement*, was surprisingly irenic in response to such hostile treatment. He attempts to respond to Martineau's criticisms and does not mention the rather rough handling he had received in the review.

70. *The Nature of the Atonement*, p. 401.

71. *The Nature of the Atonement*, p. 403.

72. *The Nature of the Atonement*, p. 378.

73. He repeats this belief in this same section, "As to these deepest facts of our being and of our relation to God, I have not even attempted to determine the line that separates the darkness and the light. . ." *The Nature of the Atonement*, p. 376.

74. A critical note to Campbell's theory arises naturally here. Campbell's atonement theology is "Trinitarianily weighted" on the side of the Father and the Son. The two concepts of Fatherhood and Sonship are major constitutive parts in Campbell's theology. Although the Holy Spirit makes an appearance, even an important appearance, here and there in Campbell's book, discussion of the Spirit is minimal. Here, in the question of the relationship between Christ and the believer, more complete consideration of the person and work of the Holy Spirit may well have been helpful and illuminating to Campbell.

75. "This relation, whether we contemplate it as participation in our flesh, or as that relation to us in the spirit in respect of which Christ is our life, having power over all flesh to this end, is indeed a mystery as to its *nature* and *manner*, and to be known by us only in its *results*" (p. 377).

76. He insists on the divinity of Christ on p. 379, *The Nature of the Atonement*, "I believe, as I have said, that the faith of the atonement, and the faith that we have eternal life in Christ, is more easy to us when it rests on the faith of the divinity of Christ."

77. *The Nature of the Atonement*, p. 127.

78. *The Nature of the Atonement*, p. xxvii.

79. *The Nature of the Atonement*, p. 127. Emphasis mine.

80. *The Nature of the Atonement*, p. 377, "This relation, whether we contemplate it as participation in our flesh, or as that relation to us in the spirit in respect of which Christ is our life, having power over all flesh to his end, is indeed a mystery as to its **nature** and **manner**, and to be known by us only in its **results**." This theme finds voice in other writings of Campbell as well. Cf. *Christ the Bread of Life* (London: Macmillan & Co., 1869), p. 184, where Campbell says in his usual opaque style, "Eternal Life in Christian vindicates its claim to identify with the Eternal Life in Christ by its living response to Christ's words. When as the revealer of the Father our Lord invites men as weary and heavy laden to come to Him for rest; to take His yoke and learn of Him who is meek and lowly in heart; the divine consciousness of the Son in humanity following the Father as a dear child

which utters itself in the words, 'My yoke is easy, and my burden is light' awakens a living echo in all who through Him are partaking in the life of sonship, and following God as dear children walking in love."

81. Campbell, *Christ the Bread of Life*, p. 83. Campbell briefly alludes, in the context of Christ's relationship of obedience to the Father, to "our Lord's uniform intimation of a parallelism between His own relation to the Father and our relation to Himself. . ."

82. This is the version of the Galatians 2:20 passage that Campbell quotes.

83. *The Nature of the Atonement*, p. 404. Emphasis mine.

84. *The Nature of the Atonement*, p. 334, "The work of Christ, while of infinite excellence in itself, has its special value as the work of redemption in the excellence of its result . . . this divine excellence in humanity in the person of Christ is seen as in humanity with a view to results in all humanity." Cf. Goodloe, p. 90.

85. *The Nature of the Atonement*, p. 403.

86. *The Nature of the Atonement*, p. 178.

CHAPTER FIVE

CAMPBELL AND THE REFORMED TRADITION: CONTINUITIES WITH CALVIN

The coherence and completeness of Campbell's atonement theology has been established in the chapters above by an examination of the content of Campbell's atonement theology and an inquiry into a number of specific difficulties. But Campbell's contribution to the broader Reformed tradition has yet to be described. Campbell's own contribution to the tradition of Reformed theology will be demonstrated in the significant conceptual connections between John Calvin and John McLeod Campbell. The rationale for this continuity claim may not initially be clear. After all, Campbell scarcely mentions Calvin in *The Nature of the Atonement*. He expressly shows a higher regard for Luther than for Calvin.[1] Why, then, is continuity with Calvin an issue?

In order to answer that question, some reflection on the role of Calvin in the broader Reformed tradition is necessary. Calvin scholarship in recent decades has established the diverse character of early Reformed theology.[2] Although certainly Calvin remains the most influential and important of sixteenth century Reformed theologians, the origins, as well as subsequent development, of the Reformed tradition are nuanced and complex.

To specify this early diversity in the Reformed tradition, historical theologians sometimes distinguish two streams of early Reformed theology, the one called "Calvinist" and the other called "federalist" or "covenantal." Points of dispute arise in trying to determine which sixteenth century theologians belong properly to which group. One scholar claims the Calvinist stream includes Zwingli, Bucer, Peter Martyr, and Calvin. The federalist stream includes Oecolampadius, Capito, Bullinger, and Tyndale.[3] But other historical theologians compile quite different lists, placing in the federalist category only a few, notably Bullinger and Tyndale, and others in the broad Calvinist stream, which itself admits of multiple divisions, such as scholastic Calvinism.[4] Another scheme might be that Calvin's own unique contribution be identified as "Calvinian," the scholastics of the seventeenth and eighteenth centuries as "Calvinists," those with debts to Bullinger as "federalists," as well as other possible permutations such as "Puritan" and "Edwardsean."

Lines of continuity in the Reformed tradition are, thus, complex and diverse. The relevance of this complexity of origins for interpreters of John McLeod Campbell is in attempting to determine primary dependencies and continuities of Campbell's own theology. It will be recalled that Campbell strongly countered the emphases of the federalist, or covenantal, framework of Scottish Presbyterian theology. Because he saw unhappy pastoral effects of an emphasis on limited atonement and the practical syllogism as the basis for an assurance of faith, Campbell sought a new basis and foundation for his theology, namely, love as the primary attribute of God. He avoided positing legal obligations on God based on God's justice. Thus, his rejection of legal or juridical atonement categories places him firmly in opposition to that stream of Reformed theology which significantly employs legal and juridical categories, especially exemplified by federalist and scholastic Reformed theologies. But Campbell's explicit rejection of one particular stream of the Reformed tradition does not dismiss him from the broader tradition. The question is if Campbell can legitimately be included in one or another of the major streams in the Reformed tradition, perhaps one with stronger ties to Calvin or exhibiting continuity with important themes in Calvin.

Investigating Campbell's conceptual continuity with Calvin is a promising approach to understanding Campbell's obligations to the broad Reformed tradition. Although Campbell neither rejected nor claimed Calvin as his theological forbear, the question is at least intriguing. Since Campbell so clearly distanced himself from one major stream of Reformed theology, the federalist stream strongly characterized by certain legal metaphors and a particular view of God's justice, is it possible that Campbell aligned himself with another major stream of Reformed theology, namely, the Calvinian stream?

There are other reasons why such continuity is worth exploration. As has been noted in previous chapters, critical reception of Campbell has tended to various reductionistic renderings of his atonement theology. Conservative or evangelical theologians have judged Campbell to be regrettably subjective in his atonement reflection. Other interpreters, making essentially the same analysis, celebrate the supposed subjective nature of Campbell's atonement reflection.[5] This typical judgement on Campbell is mistaken; in fact, Campbell's atonement theology is a successful and coherent balance of objective and subjective elements.[6] Thus to investigate Campbell's continuity with Calvin furthers the goal of an accurate appraisal of Campbell's own theology. For it can hardly be claimed that Calvin is simply a subjectivist in his atonement reflections. To link Campbell with Calvin on significant atonement questions would aid in correcting an old misunderstanding of Campbell's atonement theology.

An additional reason why a continuity investigation between Calvin and Campbell is useful is that such demonstrated continuity will enhance and strengthen the Reformed tradition. Campbell's own unique and particular contribution to atonement theology is weighty and important; the possibility of a significant connection between Calvin and Campbell thus becomes auspicious.

It is not necessary, or possible, to match Campbell with Calvin at every point of comparison. Indeed, it is quite possible for Campbell to differ from Calvin on many minor and several major issues and still establish significant continuity. Neither it is necessary for this chapter to enter the heated discussion on whether Campbell was a "Calvinist" or whether, in fact, Calvin was a "Calvinist."[7]

This chapter will demonstrate important and meaningful continuity between the atonement accounts of John Calvin and John McLeod Campbell. It will not be claimed that the two theories are continuous in all respects. Differences, even weighty differences, exist between the two accounts. Rather, the continuity will be claimed on the basis of evidence along two fronts. First, it will be shown that the fundamental principles or presuppositions of both Calvin and Campbell are similar with respect to the atonement. Second, it will be demonstrated that vital themes in Calvin that were muted in the

Reformed tradition as Campbell received it in federalist nineteenth century Scottish theology were reclaimed and strengthened in Campbell's account of the atonement.

As a result of this investigation, it will be confirmed that Campbell's continuity with Calvin is important both for an accurate reading of Campbell as well as an accurate reading of Calvin. That is to say, the continuity demonstrated alters significantly the small tradition of critical analysis on Campbell and alters, as well, the long tradition of critical analysis on Calvin. This conclusion refutes those interpreters of Campbell already surveyed who dismiss his theology as typical of nineteenth century liberal or subjectivist theologies. Rather, Campbell proves to be an example of the diversity and vitality of the ongoing tradition of distinctively Reformed theological reflection.

Continuity of Presuppositions in Calvin and Campbell

There are, of course, significant areas of similarity and continuity between Calvin and Campbell that will not be examined here. By virtue of the fact that they are both Christian theologians working in the Western tradition of the church, Calvin and Campbell have in common wide expanses of shared vision. The intent in what follows is to highlight several key areas of continuity that serve to demonstrate Campbell's authentic connection with Calvin.

An initial line of continuity from Calvin to Campbell is a shared methodological emphasis; both thinkers perceive all of God's gracious activity in the atonement by focusing first, and always, on Jesus Christ. Calvin puts it this way, "If, then, we would be assured that God is pleased with and kindly disposed toward us, we must fix our eyes and minds on Christ alone."[8] For Campbell, this is a familiar theme. The title of chapter 5 in *The Nature of the Atonement* says just this, that the atonement must be "seen by its own light." That is to say, in considering the atonement, one must not begin with abstract questions such as, "What is an atonement for sin?" but rather, "it is surely wise to seek its answer in the study of the atonement for sin actually made, and revealed to our faith as accepted by God."[9] For both Calvin and Campbell, a fuller understanding of the atonement comes from believing it and believing that

Christ accomplished it through Christ.

The methodological approach to the atonement of both Calvin and Campbell begins with faith, not with an historical fact which then requires interpretation. Atonement theology does not take a bare fact and history and impose a soteriological explanation. Rather, it begins with the soteriological event of Christ's atoning death and then seeks discernment and systematic understanding.[10]

The presupposition or guiding principle common to both Calvin and Campbell with respect to atonement theology is the emphasis on the love of God as the divine motivation for the atonement and as the overarching divine disposition toward humanity throughout the events of the atoning life, death, and resurrection of Jesus Christ. That this is a crucial presupposition for John McLeod Campbell no one will question. His early Row sermons aroused the suspicions of a few of his parishioners precisely on this point; they felt he talked entirely too much about the love of God. Campbell's letters to family and friends attest as well to his continual reflection on the love of God. Most importantly for this study, *The Nature of the Atonement* clearly and repeatedly emphasizes the love of God as both the foundation and the content of the atoning work of Christ.[11]

The love of God is also a crucial presupposition for the atonement theology of John Calvin. Although it is common for accounts of the history of atonement theory to stress more Calvin's emphasis on the penal and judicial aspects of atonement, it is clear both in the *Institutes* as well as Calvin's commentaries that the free and gracious love of God is the starting point for all further thought on the atoning work of Christ. L.W. Grensted, in his usually accurate study on the history of atonement theology, provides a typical example of long-standing reductionist perceptions among historical theologians that Calvin's atonement contributions were dominated by justice and punishment concerns. Grensted says, "Like the other Reformers, he (Calvin) follows the Anselmic method, modified by the aspect of justice as avenging, demanding punishment for sin in its own right."[12] Grensted does quickly admit that Calvin is not "unmindful of the love of God," but such a concession to what is actually the foundational presupposition of Calvin's theology is not adequate to right the balance of careful and fair perception on Calvin's theology. Numerous other examples are readily available to illustrate this old mistake with respect to Calvin's theology.[13]

It is not difficult to see that the origin of this lopsided interpretation of Calvin's theology is the assumption that Calvin and the Calvinists represent one univocal, monolithic tradition. It is certainly true that several streams of the Calvinists, notably the covenantal and scholastic streams, explicitly muted the love of God in favor of the justice of God as primary divine attribute. But federal Calvinism's atonement account should not be equated with Calvin's atonement account.

Calvin's commentaries speak of the love of God with a simplicity and frequency that Campbell surely would have heartily endorsed. "The ground of our redemption is that immense love of God towards us by which it happened that He did not even spare His own Son."[14] "For it is not true (as some carelessly make out) that repentance is put in first place, as though it were the cause of the remission of sins, or came before God's starting to be well-favoured towards us, but men are told to repent that they may perceive the reconciliation that is offered to them. As first in rank comes the free love of God, in which He embraces poor men, not imputing their sins to them."[15] "Christ is such a shining and remarkable proof of the divine love towards us, that, whenever we look to Him, He clearly confirms to us the doctrine that God is love."[16]

The organization of Calvin's atonement theology in the *Institutes*, admittedly, obscures his emphasis on the love of God.[17] Not only the organization, but the repeated emphasis of Calvin on the wrath of God in Book II can perhaps serve to dim the glow of God's love as primary divine attribute in the work of the atonement. Yet Calvin's extended treatment of God's wrath and hostility is primarily pedagogical, intended to highlight how great humanity's peril is and how greater God's love is.[18] Indeed, Calvin's whole point in the organization of Book II is that God's love is most dramatically displayed and highlighted only after a full and sober realization of the depth and extent of human sin.[19]

But after explicating human sin and God's just reaction of wrath against such sin in much of Book II, Calvin then says, "Therefore, by his love God the Father goes before and anticipates our reconciliation in Christ."[20] Again, he states,

> The fact that we were reconciled through Christ's death must not be understood as if his Son reconciled us to him that he might now begin to love those whom he had hated. Rather, we have already been reconciled to him who loves us, with whom we were enemies on account of sin. Therefore, he loved us even when we practiced enmity toward him and committed wickedness.[21]

Calvin's discussion of the relationship between the justice or wrath of God and the mercy or love of God is more complex than these brief quotes can indicate. These complications in Calvin's argument do not cancel the force of the claim that his foundational principle is the love of God, but they do nuance the argument. Calvin struggles with the problem of the logical progression of human guilt, divine wrath, divine love, forgiveness, satisfaction and reconciliation. In that struggle, he says things like, "For, in some ineffable way, God loved us and yet was angry toward us at the same time, until he became reconciled to us in Christ"[22] or, "Thus in a marvelous and divine way he loved us even when he hated us."[23] Such statements arise from the fact that Calvin wants to take with utmost seriousness the truth that God really hates sin; God does not just pretend to hate sin in order to lure sinners to repentance. But he also wants to take with utmost seriousness the truth that God always bridges the chasm between Godself and humanity with redemptive love and gracious intent. Calvin's attempt to understand the relationship between God's love and God's wrath rests finally in a combination of ideas: his notion of God accommodating Godself to our inadequate capacities,[24] his idea of mystery or "some ineffable way" that God alone understands,[25] and, most importantly, his ultimate confidence in God's overarching love. In spite of Calvin's efforts to understand what he perceives to be a difficult and complex problem between God's love and God's anger, he is assured that, "We see how God's love holds first place, as the highest cause or origin. . ."[26]

Continuity between Campbell and Calvin on the fundamental presupposition of God's love as primary divine attribute and motivation for the atonement is important both for a reassessment of Campbell's theology as well as a reassessment of Calvin's theology. Campbell, it will be recalled, was criticized by those in his day, and by some subsequent interpreters, by emphasizing too much the love of God. Calvin has often been dismissed by interpreters who tend to read Calvin through the lens of the Calvinist tradition for his lack of attention to the love of God in favor of what has been seen as more dominant categories such as the justice of God or divine election.

A convincing continuity claim helps to clear both these theologians from unfortunate misunderstanding. The demonstration that Campbell's theology, constructed on the principle of the overarching love of God, is not a subjectively liberal or thinly moralistic system but rather a significant continuation of the theology of Calvin, at least with respect to basic presuppositions, is a much needed corrective in Campbell studies. Likewise, a demonstration that Calvin's theology is not identical to subsequent scholastic and covenantal developments which often muted themes of the love of God is a much needed corrective in Calvin studies.

Continuity in Retrospective Themes in Calvin and Campbell

The retrospective aspect of the atonement denoted for Campbell the remission of sins. "Retrospective" is a near-synonym to an "objective" account of the atonement, that is, an account that focuses on Christ's life, death, and resurrection as accomplishing in a certain time and place broad salvific effects, including the reconciliation between God and humanity and the basis for a forgiveness of sins, past and future. For Campbell, these retrospective benefits were accomplished by Christ's perfect response to God's condemnation of sin and Christ perfectly witnessing to humanity of the love of God and God's sorrow over sin.[27]

Calvin's terminology bears scant resemblance to Campbell's admittedly idiosyncratic images and terms. His atonement account, as evidenced in the *Institutes*, uses categories of Christ as Mediator, Christ as Prophet, Priest, and King, Christ as our substitute, the satisfaction of Christ's sacrifice, and Christ as earning the merit for our salvation. The range of images and themes in Calvin's account of the atonement is diverse. It has often been assumed that the images of penalty, punishment, and propitiation are the dominating atonement images in Calvin. But a careful reading of the whole of Book II of the *Institutes* instead supports the theory that the image of sacrifice, discussed by Calvin in his section on the priestly work of Christ, is the primary organizing image, not punishment.[28]

Christ is the sacrifice for sin, according to Calvin, so that satisfaction be made to God. In a key passage in the *Institutes*, Calvin explains the purpose of the priestly office of Christ, "Thus Christ to perform this office had to come forward with a sacrifice. . . The priestly office belongs to Christ alone because by the sacrifice of his death he blotted out our own guilt and made satisfaction for our sins."[29] Thus, atonement is effected, according to Calvin, in that satisfaction is rendered to God for the offense of sin by means of the sacrifice of Christ's death.

Equally important to the concept that Christ made satisfaction for our sins by the sacrifice of his death is that Christ made satisfaction as well through the course of his obedient life. Although Calvin does not use the term "satisfaction" with reference to Christ's obedience, the obedience of Christ is clearly a parallel concept in his argument. He says, "Now some ask, 'How has Christ abolished sin, banished the separation between us and God, and acquired righteousness to render God favorable and kindly toward us?' "[30] This question asks, in effect, "How is satisfaction made to God for sin?" His answer, immediately following the question, is, "To this we can in general reply that he has achieved this for us by the whole course of his obedience." Calvin elaborates this point, employing a number of Scriptural citations in its defense,

> In short, from the time when he took on the form of a servant, he began to pay the price of liberation in order to redeem us. . . And we must hold fast to this: that no proper sacrifice to God could have been offered unless Christ, disregarding his own feelings, subjected and yielded himself wholly to his Father's will.[31]

Calvin then adds the rather surprising remark that so much emphasis is placed on the sacrificial death of Christ in accommodation to human weakness. "But because trembling consciences find repose only in sacrifice and cleansing by which sins are expiated, we are duly directed thither; and for us the substance of life is set in the death of Christ." His point seems to be that both the death of Christ as a sacrifice satisfies God and the obedience of Christ in his earthly life satisfies God. The focus, due to our "trembling consciences," is on the death of Christ.

Robert Paul, noting Calvin's view of Christ's obedience as a "central atoning principle," laments the heavy emphasis in Calvin on penal satisfaction,

> Had he held closely to this insight and seen it as the center of what he was trying to say about Christ's work for us, he would not only have avoided overconcentration upon punitive ideas which did not honor the God he wanted to honor, but he would have shown that sacrifice is at the heart of the biblical idea of the atonement, and that the sacrifice offered by Christ was a total sacrifice of the whole life which culminates in His death and is vindicated in His resurrection.[32]

Robert Paul's regret over the relative emphasis in Calvin on penal aspects of the atonement is precisely that the real center of Calvin's atonement theology lies elsewhere - in the whole obedient life of Christ offered to God as a sacrifice which effected full satisfaction.

For Calvin, the central atonement concept is the satisfaction Christ made to God through an obedient life and a sacrificial death. The point of similarity and continuity with Campbell is precisely in the idea of satisfaction. For Campbell too, Christ made satisfaction to the Father. The details of satisfaction in the accounts of Calvin and Campbell differ, but the essential point of satisfaction in the two accounts is similar, that is, the obedient life and sacrificial death of Christ made possible and complete reconciliation between God and humanity.[33]

Campbell himself did not designate his atonement theology as a satisfaction account. Such a framework did not occur to him. After all, Campbell's critique of the standard Calvinist satisfaction atonement accounts, either scholastic or federalist, were very negative.[34] Both the scholastic or Puritan accounts, like that of John Owen, or the federalist accounts, like those of his contemporaries or near-contemporaries in Scotland, used the framework of satisfaction in the sense of penalty or punishment. Campbell expended all his critical energies in *The Nature of the Atonement* refuting these atonement accounts which focus so heavily on penal accounts of satisfaction. Thus, he did not consider that perhaps the basic concept of satisfaction might be retained in his atonement exposition but the terms of satisfaction altered.

But, in effect, this is precisely what Campbell accomplishes in his account of the atonement. The retrospective core of Campbell's account, namely, Christ's perfect confession, is an alternate form of a satisfaction account of the atonement. Richard Swinburne, in his careful and convincing book on the basic elements of atonement theory, makes the point with respect to satisfaction that there may be a variety of ways to render satisfaction to the offended party.[35] The Reformed tradition has focused almost exclusively on penal substitution as the means of satisfaction. But Campbell presents an option to a penal substitution account of a satisfaction theory in his perfect confession account of a satisfaction theory. On this theory, Christ makes satisfaction to the Father by making a perfect confession to God, a confession both of the outrage of sin and the complete righteousness of the Father's condemnation of sin. Through this confession, Christ "absorbed" the wrath of God.

It was claimed in chapter four, above, that this interesting concept of absorption is a key concept in Campbell's account. It was also noted that Campbell could not, within the confines of his theory, say much more about how Christ's confession absorbs God's wrath. It did not occur to Campbell that perhaps he was formulating a satisfaction theory with different terms of satisfaction than the tradition had displayed. Now, in the context of comparing Campbell's account with Calvin's satisfaction account, it can be seen that Campbell's use of the concept of absorption of God's wrath is, in effect, a way of expressing a theory of satisfaction. Because of Christ's perfect confession of humanity's sin and perfect acknowledgement of God's righteousness condemnation of sin, **God is satisfied** and the way is open for full reconciliation. Campbell's own phrase, that "God's wrath is absorbed," is an evocative expression of a basic satisfaction account. The terms differ from Calvin's satisfaction account, but the central core of the two accounts are remarkably similar. The idea of satisfaction underlies both Calvin's and Campbell's atonement theologies.

There are several intriguing aspects of this point of continuity between Calvin and Campbell. For one, Campbell himself, as briefly noted above, did not indicate his awareness that his theory was a variant of a basic satisfaction account. Yet, he hinted at that awareness in his discussion of Christ's confession:

> I have endeavoured to present Christ's expiatory confession of our sins to the mind of the reader as much as possible by itself, and as a distinct object of thought, because it most directly corresponds, in the place it occupies, to the penal suffering which has been assumed; and I have desired to place these two ways of meeting the divine wrath against sin, as ascribed to the Mediator, in contrast.[36]

In another place, Campbell gives a hint that perhaps he was somewhat aware that his theory was a variant of a satisfaction account. He says, "Nor is the idea that satisfaction was due to divine justice a delusion, however far men have wandered from the true conception of what would meet its righteous demand."[37] Here Campbell rightly observes that satisfying the righteous demand of God must not necessarily entail penal substitution. But he does not fully recognize this feature of his own theology and its important connection with the tradition of which he was a part. Campbell knew that his theory of Christ's perfect confession was in contrast to penal substitution and, further, that the two theories both described a "way of meeting the divine wrath against sin," but he did not consider that his concept of Christ's perfect confession was basically a variant of a satisfaction account.

Another intriguing aspect of this point of continuity between Calvin and Campbell is that this feature of Campbell's atonement theology, namely, that its retrospective aspect is a variant of a satisfaction theory, is routinely missed by Campbell interpreters. It has been pointed out several times that interpretive reaction to Campbell's atonement theology has tended toward either dismay over what is perceived as a subjective, moral influence theory or relief over the same perception.[38] The possibility that Campbell's atonement theology presents a modified version of a satisfaction atonement theory has not been considered by Campbell interpreters.

Continuity between Calvin and Campbell with respect to the retrospective aspect of the atonement also significantly exists in a shared concept of the obedient life of Christ as a means of satisfaction. This important feature of Calvin's theology was noted above, a feature that was muted in subsequent development in the Reformed tradition in an emphasis on penal substitution. Campbell reclaimed and enlarged the theme of the obedient life of Christ as an important, even central, part of the atonement. It is a theme that appears throughout *The Nature of the Atonement*. But it figures prominently in Campbell's discussion on the retrospective aspect of the atonement. The obedient life of Christ, or the sonship of Christ, or "His love and His trust towards His Father, His love and His long suffering towards His brethren," Campbell identifies as "part of the self-sacrifice of Christ."[39] The earthly ministry of Jesus, the way Jesus related with other persons, the obedience of Jesus to the Father's will - all these were elements of Christ's sacrifice and were effective in making satisfaction to God.

There is no question that the atonement accounts of Calvin and Campbell contain significant differences as well. Calvin places far greater emphasis on Christ bearing the guilt and punishment for our sins. In fact, in the section immediately following his discussion of the obedient life of Christ, Calvin states, "This is our acquittal: the guilt that held us liable for punishment has been transferred to the head of the Son of God. We must, above all, remember this substitution lest we tremble and remain anxious throughout life - as if God's righteous vengeance, which the Son of God has taken upon himself, still hung over us."[40]   Campbell simply does not use language like this. For Campbell, Christ's sufferings were not substituted punishment for the offense of sin but rather a natural and unavoidable part of Christ's witnessing to the holiness and love of God.

Fully acknowledging the key differences between Calvin and Campbell in their atonement reflections does not cancel the important points of continuity indicated above, namely, that both theologians use a form of a satisfaction account and that both theologians see the obedient life of Christ as a part of the sacrifice, a part of making satisfaction to God.

Continuity in Prospective Themes in Calvin and Campbell

It is the prospective aspect of the atonement where the most striking and compelling areas of continuity emerge between Calvin and Campbell. This section will identify and demonstrate these important continuities between the two theologians.

One line of continuity in the prospective aspect of the atonement between Calvin and Campbell is a shared emphasis on the continual intercession of Christ before the Father. Calvin is clear that Christ's mediatorial work continues after his ascension on our behalf. In the context of a discussion on prayer, Calvin says that Christ is "the only way, and the only access, by which it is granted us to come to God."[41]   Quoting I John 2:1, Calvin adds the rhetorical question, "For when John says, 'If anyone sins, we have an advocate with the Father, Christ Jesus', does he mean that Christ was an advocate for us once for all, or does he not rather ascribe to him a constant intercession?"[42]

In Campbell's small treatise on Christian worship, he too says that our prayers are in Christ's name, who is always honoring the Father on our behalf.[43] He further develops the theme in his discussion on the prospective aspect of the atonement. In the context of emphasizing that Christ's self-sacrifice has broad implications for the Christian life, Campbell says, "Therefore Christ, as the Lord of our spirits and our life, **devotes us to God** and **devotes us to men** in the **fellowship of His self-sacrifice**."[44]   He adds that, at the same time that Christ is giving us the gift of fellowship with brothers and sisters in the faith, he is also commending and devoting us to God. Campbell's point is that the gift of adopted sonship is closely related to the gift of brotherly fellowship. One cannot be rich in the first without being rich in the second.[45] Thus, the continuing activity of Christ on our behalf has effect both in heaven before the Father as well as on earth within the community of faith.

The most important area of continuity between Calvin and Campbell is their use of the concept of union with Christ. Some Calvin scholars consider union with Christ to be the central theological concept of Calvin's theology.[46] Even those who are reluctant to identify union with Christ as the center of Calvin's theology admit its importance. Kolfhaus, who produced a classic full length study on this theme said, "I do not mean that the doctrine of union with Christ represents the central doctrine of Calvin; but that it gives us much important information about many things, indeed the most significant areas of Calvinist thought."[47] Many other Calvin scholars agree. E. Brunner, like Kolfhaus, said union with Christ is "the center of all Calvinist thought"; David Willis-Watkins identifies union with Christ in Calvin as "one of the most consistently influential features of his theology and ethics, if not indeed the whole of his thought and his personal life"; and P.J. Richel affirmed that "for Calvin the concept of the *unio mystica* is of fundamental importance for his entire theological thought."[48]

The search for the organizing principle of Calvin's theology has a long history. In 1938, Niesel lamented that, "Calvin research suffers from the defect that the golden thread which runs through it has not yet been discovered. . . what is really in question when he writes his *Institutes of the Christian Religion*, what his governing intention is in constructing his theology, remains as yet unknown to us."[49] Niesel identified several prevailing options, at that time, with respect to the foundation of Calvin's theological system, including the gracious God,[50] the justice of God or predestination,[51] sanctification,[52] the honor of God,[53] and God incarnate in Jesus Christ.[54] In the context of new Calvin research which has rendered these foci as dated or at least incomplete, Willis-Watkins has perhaps suggested the most accurate as well as most modest claim with respect to union with

Christ, namely, that it is a doctrine of significant and consistent influence in his entire theological reflection.

In seeking to explicate the meaning of union with Christ in Calvin's theology, it is important to recognize the diversity of expression that Calvin himself employs. Krusche compiled a list of key phrases that appear in Calvin's commentaries and in the *Institutes*, phrases which include *unio cum Christum, insertio in Christum, coalescere cum Christo, participatio cum Christo, and habitatio Christi in nobis*.[55] Calvin also occasionally uses the phrase *unio mystica*.[56] These phrases, although differing in root metaphor and nuance, all denote the relationship between Christ and the believing person.

Calvin captured the essence of this relationship memorably when he said, "First, we must understand that as long as Christ remains outside of us, and we are separated from him, all that he   suffered and done for the salvation of the human race remains useless and of no value for us."[57] Thus, it is necessary for the believer to be united to Christ by the bond of the Holy Spirit through faith. "To sum up, the Holy Spirit is the bond by which Christ effectually unites us to himself."[58] By this, Calvin means a spiritual union, not a confusion of substance as Calvin understood Osiander to posit, but certainly an intimate and complete union.[59] He says in one of his sermons, "In this sense, then, let us know the unity that we have with our Lord Jesus Christ; to wit, that he wills to have a common life with us, and that what he has should be ours: nay, that he even wishes to dwell in us, not in imagination, but in effect; not in earthly fashion but spiritually; and that whatever may befall, he so labours by the virtue of his Holy Spirit that we are united with him more closely than are the limbs with the body."[60]

The union between Christ and the believer is a bond that grows as faith grows, according to Calvin. He says, ". . . with a wonderful communion, day by day, he grows more and more into one body with us. . ."[61] Moreover, because of that union, we are participants with Christ and heirs with Christ of God's kingdom.[62] This status as redeemed people united with Christ gives the Christian community the freedom and the call to live in such a way that Christ is imitated, God is glorified, and the Spirit is manifest. It is, in short, the foundation for Christian ethics.

Another aspect of union with Christ, according to Calvin, is that this bond between Christ and the believer is so complete, that the believer can actually share in Christ's sacrifice as well as in Christ's salvific benefits.[63] This is not a strongly developed theme in Calvin, but it does appear in Book II of the *Institutes* where he says, "Now, Christ plays the priestly role, not only to render the Father favorable and propitious toward us by an eternal law of reconciliation, but also **to receive us as his companions in this great office.** For we who are defiled in ourselves, yet are priests in him, offer ourselves and our all to God, and freely enter the heavenly sanctuary. . ."[64] Thus, in some sense, the believer imitates the sacrifice of Christ in her own life of worship and service; in some sense, the believer is, through being united with Christ, a part in Christ's sacrifice; in some sense, the believer enters into Christ's work of salvation. So encompassing is Calvin's notion of union with Christ that even the great moments of salvation and redemption accomplished by Christ are shared by the believing community through the work of the Holy Spirit.

It is clear from this brief overview that the doctrine of union with Christ is an extraordinarily evocative, encompassing concept for Calvin, a concept that can be identified as central in Calvin's theology. It not only specifies the relationship between Christ and the believer through faith, but also implies the assurance of faith, the shape of an ethical life, and the sharing by believers of the sacrifice of Christ.

Union with Christ is an equally evocative and encompassing theme in the atonement theology of John McLeod Campbell. Campbell's terminology focuses primarily on the imagery of adoption, of participation in Christ, and of partaking in the mind of Christ. Union with Christ is a central theme in Campbell's prospective aspect of the atonement, one that has many connections to ethics, the assurance of faith, and the life of the believing community. In this, Campbell is in impressive continuity with Calvin.

Campbell's discussion of union with Christ is located in the context of the prospective aspect of the atonement, that is, what effects the atonement of Christ has for the present and the future.

Campbell, typically, does not clearly explicate the contours of this doctrine. Rather, it appears as an integral and essential part of everything he has to say about the effects of Christ's work.

He says, for instance, that Christ's perfect confession of our sins not only absorbed God's wrath and fully acknowledged God's judgement against sin, but it also must ". . . have contemplated prospectively **our own participation in that confession** as an element in our actual redemption from sin."[65] Furthermore, through the saving work of Christ, Christ now wishes that all people "**partake in His own life** in the Father's favour."[66]2 Other ideas include "a participation in the mind and life of Christ" as a benefit or reward of redemption,[67] and humanity's "inestimable preciousness . . . is indeed not to be contemplated as belonging to us apart from **our relation to the Son of God.**"[68]

By contrasting his own view with what he perceives as the grave weaknesses of any legal atonement account, Campbell more completely explains the bond between Christ and the believer,

> Therefore, there must be a relation between the Son of God and the sons of men, not according to the flesh only, but also according to the spirit . . . But if we see this double relation subsisting between Christ and men, if we see Him as the Lord of their spirits, as well as a partaker in their flesh, that air of legal fiction, which in contemplating the atonement, attaches to our identification with Christ and Christ's identification with us, so long as this is contemplated as a matter of external arrangement, will pass away, and the **depth and reality of the bonds which connect the Saviour and the saved** will bear the weight of this identification. . .[69]

By this extended quote, Campbell is claiming that the relationship between Christ and the believer is best perceived not as an external, legal arrangement but rather as an intimate bond between the body and spirit of Christ and the bodies and spirits of believers. Campbell's images in his explication of union with Christ, typical of his theology as a whole, are organic and wholistic rather than atomistic and mechanical.

T.F. Torrance has demonstrated the importance of Campbell's doctrine of union with Christ and has shown the wide-ranging impact of this doctrine to related matters.[70] For example, Campbell's view of the relation between Christ and the believer in faith illuminates Christian worship as "properly a form of the life of Jesus Christ ascending to the Father in the life of those who are so intimately related to him through the Spirit, that when they pray to the Father through Christ, it is Christ the Incarnate Son who honours, worships and glorifies the Father in them."[71] In Christian worship, "it is the mind of Christ which we present to the Father."[72] More clearly, he writes in a letter to his oldest son, "If it is true that 'we live; yet not we, but Christ in us,' it is true that we offer ourselves as living sacrifices; yet not we, but Christ in us. For what does God accept as our true worship? Is it not Christ?"[73] For Campbell, one specific manifestation of union with Christ in the life of the believer is the act of prayer, and worship. More generally, the whole life of faith "is an abiding in and a living by Christ as he abides in and lives by the Father."[74]

A related line of continuity between Calvin and Campbell with respect to union with Christ has to do with believers having a share of or a part in the sacrifice of Christ. This was seen briefly, but significantly, in Calvin.[75] Campbell, too, says that, "the sinner enters in the Amen of faith . . . to Christ's confession of our sins. . . we receive strength to say Amen to it - to join in it. . ."[76] Again, he says, in reference to Christ's sacrifice, "We see further that what is thus offered on our behalf is so offered by the Son and so accepted by the Father, entirely with the prospective purpose that it is to be reproduced in us."[77]

It can be seen by the above citations from Campbell that, although his concept of union with Christ is not as explicitly developed as Calvin's treatment of this central concept, it is of decisive importance in his atonement theology. It is the "depth and reality of the bonds which connect the Saviour and the saved" that our salvation is assured, that we are actually included in the work of Christ, that our worship is authenticated, and that our status as well-loved adopted sons and daughters is demonstrated.

Calvin and Campbell differ in their emphasis on the divine persons in their concepts of union and sonship. Campbell tends to emphasize the ultimate relation between the believer and the Father; Calvin emphasizes the relation between the believer and Christ. This is not surprising, given Campbell's strong foundational principle that the goal of the atonement is to restore the lost sinner to the Father's love. It is that relationship of the loving Father to the restored sinner that Cambpell sees not only as the root of the atonement, but also its goal.[78] He states, "The Son of God saves us by a work whose essence and sum is the declaring of the Father's name,"[79] and asks rhetorically, "Reader, let me ask you, do you pray as a child of God whose first and nearest relationship is to God your Father. . .?"[80]

For Campbell, in short, the essence of salvation is sonship; ". . . our salvation shall be participation in the life of sonship."[81] But this emphasis on the goal of salvation being a restored relationship with the loving heart of God should not obscure the Christological focus of Campbell's work. Clearly, it is the person and work of Christ that is the possibility and fulfillment of the goal of salvation. Campbell explicitly links the life of sonship with the saving work of Christ, "For in the Son it is, and not apart from the Son, that we have the life of sonship; and as to exercise confidence in the Father is to confide in Him as our Father, so to exercise confidence in the Son is to welcome the life of sonship which we have in Him."[82]

Summary

This survey of the lines of continuity between Calvin and Campbell has included some of the most central and important themes of any atonement theology. Noteworthy presuppositional similarities between Calvin and Campbell include a shared methodological approach based on faith and a guiding principle which focuses on the love of God.

Significant continuities in the retrospective aspect of the atonement is the satisfaction accounts in both Calvin and Campbell. Terminology and imagery differ; but the foundational concept of Christ rendering satisfaction to God through his life and death is fundamentally similar. The differences in how Calvin and Campbell perceive the exact nature of the sacrifice of Christ and the exact nature of the satisfaction are not to be minimized; they render the two atonement theologies different in some crucial respects. But the foundational similarities do exist and it is those that this chapter has highlighted.

Notable in the prospective aspect of the atonement is the similarity in the encompassing theme of union with Christ. In addition, the continual intercession of Christ before the Father and the theme of believers sharing in the sacrifice of Christ are seen in the atonement theologies of both Calvin and Campbell.

NOTES

1. Campbell does not explain why he chooses to focus on Luther rather than on Calvin. It may be that Campbell assumes Calvin is a "Calvinist," namely, the original proponent of the position he is determined to discredit as theologically bankrupt. Or, it may be simply that Campbell is not interested in engaging important voices from the Protestant tradition, except, as in the case of Luther, if that voice can give illustration of the point he wishes to make.

2. Tony Lane, "The Quest for the Historical Calvin," *Evangelical Quarterly* 55 (1983), pp. 95-113; R.W.A. Letham, *Saving Faith and Assurance in Reformed Theology: Zwingli to the Synod of Dort*, Aberdeen Ph.D. thesis, 1979.

3. Lane, "The Quest for the Historical Calvin," p. 96, 97.

4. Charles S. McCoy and J. Wayne Baker, *Fountainhead of Federalism; Heinrich Bullinger and the Covenantal Tradition* (Louisville: Westminster/John Knox Press, 1991), pp. 21-24. Another scheme of organization of early Reformed sources is suggested by Brian Gerrish in "The Lord's Supper in the Reformed Confessions," *Theology Today* 23 (July, 1966): 224-243, where he perceives three distinct strands of the reformed tradition on the Lord's Supper.

5. Cf. especially Eugene Bewkes, in *Legacy of a Christian Mind*.

6. Recent interpreters of Campbell, such as T.F. Torrance, James Torrance, Brian Gerrish, James Goodloe, and Christian Kettler, already cited in this study, represent a new trend in Campbell interpretation that is considerably more careful and accurate in its analysis and judgement than the first century of Campbell interpretation.

7. This debate usually centers on the issue of whether Calvin held a doctrine of limited atonement or unlimited atonement. Some theologians claim that Calvin is in essential agreement with subsequent Reformed development on the doctrine of limited atonement and other theologians claim that subsequent Reformed theologians solidified a tendency in Calvin to an actual doctrine, an unfortunate and completely un-Calvinian event, according to this line of interpretation. Yet other scholars find it more important to see Calvin as himself continuous with themes or tendencies in earlier medieval theology. The literature on this extended discussion is large. For a representative sample, see Tony Lane, "The Quest for the Historical Calvin," *Evangelical Quarterly* 55 (1983), pp. 95-113, who claims the unique voice of Calvin, quite distinct either from the "Calvinists" or, more recently, the "Barthians"; the influential R.T. Kendall, *Calvin and English Calvinism to 1649* (Oxford, 1979), who sees in Calvin the doctrine of unlimited atonement and thus fundamental discontinuity with the ensuing Calvinist tradition; H. Rolston, *John Calvin versus the Westminster Confession* (Richmond, 1972) has a similar thesis as Kendall, seeing the Westminster Confession as a basic deviation from Calvin; W. Ian P. Hazlett, "The Scots Confession 1560: Context, Complexion, and Critique," *Archiv für Reformationsgeschichte* 78 (1987): 287-320, likewise examines the Scots Confession of 1560 and concludes that it is not a document of "pure Calvinism" but evidences a variety of influences and characteristics. P. Helm, "Calvin, English Calvinism and the Logic of Doctrinal Development," *Scottish Journal of Theology* 34 (1981), pp. 179-185, disagrees with Kendall and Rolston and claims essential unity between Calvin and the Calvinists on doctrinal issues; the important study by B.G. Armstrong, *Calvinism and the Amyraut Heresy* (London, 1969), and many others. This issue, of the extent of continuity between Calvin and subsequent Reformed theologians, obviously, is of great historiographic and theological importance. Here, the literature can only be briefly indicated and the issues identified.

8. John Calvin, *Institutes of the Christian Religion*, vol. 21 of *Library of Christian Classics*, ed. John T. McNeill and trans. Ford Lewis Battles (Philadelphia: Westminster Press, 1960), 2.16.3. Subsequent citations from the *Institutes* will be designated by *Institutes*, followed by book, chapter, and section numbers.

This citation from Calvin raises another important similarity between

Calvin and Campbell. That similarity is in the concept of the assurance of faith as resting in Christ, not in evidences of good works or piety. It will be recalled that this issue of assurance is what aroused the suspicions of the Church of Scotland in the 1830s over Campbell's preaching. Campbell repeatedly and insistently emphasized that a full assurance of faith, that is, a full assurance of God's love for us, is so important that it can be seen as the very essence of faith. For this claim, Campbell was deposed from the Church of Scotland. But it is a claim with strong links to Calvin's preaching and teaching. In his Romans commentary, for instance, Calvin writes, "There is, therefore, no more pernicious or destructive conception than the scholastic dogma of uncertainty of salvation" (*Comm* Rom. 8:34). Wendel also emphasizes the importance of assurance of faith for Calvin, saying that the followers of Calvin misrepresented his teaching regarding the assurance of faith. Cf. Francois Wendel, *Calvin; Origins and Development of His Religious Thought* (New York: Harper & Row, 1963), p. 277.

9. *The Nature of the Atonement*, p. 119.

10. I.U. Dalferth, in "Christ Died for Us: Reflections on the Sacrificial Language of Salvation," *Sacrifice and Redemption*, ed. S.W. Sykes, (Cambridge: Cambridge University Press, 1991) emphasizes the primacy of the soteriological event as well. "For Christians, then, the primary and basic given is not the historical fact but the soteriological event. To speak, historically, of Christ's death is in effect a partial abstraction from the full event of his dying for us. Soteriology is not an interpretative dimension of history, rather history is a perspectival narrowing of soteriology (p. 317)."

11. The claim that Campbell bases his entire theological system on the love of God was fully demonstrated in chapters one and two of this book.

12. L.W. Grensted, in *A Short History of the Doctrine of the Atonement* (Manchester: Longmans, Green, & Co., 1920), p. 209.

13. Cf., for instance, V.J.K. Brook, "The Atonement in Reformation Theology," *The Atonement in History and in Life*, ed. L.W. Grensted (London: SPCK, 1929), p. 234, where the author portrays Calvin as holding a theory of penal substitution "in its harshest form."

14. John Calvin, *The Epistle of Paul the Apostle to the Hebrews and the First and Second Epistles of St. Peter*, trans. William B. Johnston (Grand Rapids: Eerdmans Publishing Company, 1965), p. 24. Calvin is commenting here on Hebrews 2:9.

15. John Calvin, *A Harmony of the Gospels*, trans. A.W. Morrison (Edinburgh: St. Andrew's Press, 1972), p. 115. Calvin is commenting on Matthew 3:2. It is interesting to note in this passage that Calvin is fully aware of the unhappy pastoral consequences of reversing the order of grace and law, of making the love and forgiveness of God contingent on any human performance. The difficulties Campbell perceived in his congregation over the doctrine of the assurance of faith in early nineteenth century Scotland were just these that Calvin identified.

16. John Calvin, *The Gospel According to St. John 11-21 and the First Epistle of John*, trans. T.H.L. Parker, ed. T.F. Torrance and David W. Torrance (Grand Rapids: Eerdmans Publishing Company, 1961), p. 290. Calvin is commenting on I John 4:9.

17. The *Institutes*' discussion of the life and work of Christ in Book II is preceded by a thorough discussion of sin, free will, the law, the covenant, a comparison of the Old and New Testaments, and other topics of supporting or preparatory significance to the atonement.

18. *Institutes* 2.16.2, "Expressions of this sort have been accommodated to our capacity that we may better understand how miserable and ruinous our condition is apart from Christ." Later in the same section, he summarizes, ". . . we are taught by Scripture to perceive that apart from Christ, God is, so to speak, hostile to us. . ."

19. Some theologians, although recognizing the pedagogical import of Calvin's treatment of atonement, find reason to regret his starting point in the doctrine of sin and condemnation because the subsequent history of Reformed theology tended to stress too much the wrath of God and too little God's unconditional love. Cf. Paul van Buren, *Christ in our Place; the Substitutionary Character of Calvin's Doctrine of Reconciliation* (Edinburgh: Oliver and Boyd, 1957), p. 4.

20. *Institutes*, 2.16.3.

21. *Institutes*, 2.16.4.

22. *Institutes*, 2.17.2.

23. *Institutes*, 2.16.4.

24. *Institutes*, 2.16.2, "Expressions of this sort have been accommodated to our capacity that we may better understand how miserable and ruinous our condition is apart from Christ. For if it had not been clearly stated that the wrath and vengeance of God and eternal death rested upon us, we would scarcely have recognized how miserable we would have been without God's mercy, and we would have underestimated the benefit of liberation."

25. *Institutes*, 2.17.2.

26. *Institutes*, 2.17.2.

27. A complete explication of Campbell's retrospective aspect of the atonement appears above in chapters 2 and 4.

28. Calvin, *Institutes*, 2.15.6. Cf. also Robert S. Paul, "The Atonement: Sacrifice and Penalty," *Readings in Calvin's Theology*, ed. Donald K. McKim (Grand Rapids: Baker Book House, 1985), p. 146, ". . . it is the sacrificial aspect of the atonement which provides the context in which the penal ideas are set, and not the other way around." Also, Paul van Buren, *Christ in Our Place; the Substitutionary Character of Calvin's Doctrine of Reconciliation* (Edinburgh: Oliver and Boyd, 1957), pp. 73-80.

29. *Institutes*, 2.15.6.

30. *Institutes*, 2.16.5.

31. *Institutes*, 2.16.5. Cf. also 2.8.5, where Calvin suggests that God's righteousness is satisfied by obedience. He says that "nothing is more acceptable to (God) than obedience."

32. Robert S. Paul, "The Atonement: Sacrifice and Penalty," from *Readings in Calvin's Theology*, p. 151.

33. Van Buren, *Christ in Our Place*, explains that satisfaction is the summary of Calvin's atonement theology. Van Buren defines satisfaction by the general definition, "Satisfaction means that the obedient suffering of Christ in our place is completely efficacious and sufficient" (p. 76). More specifically, the satisfaction is rendered to God by means of substitution, a concept equally important for Calvin. The two concepts are related in that, "satisfaction is a way of saying what has been accomplished by substitution" (p. 78). In other words, satisfaction is the broader concept under which substitution is a specification of the means by which satisfaction is accomplished.

162

34. Cf. above, chapter 4, for Campbell's critique of the prevailing Calvinist options on atonement theories.

35. Richard Swinburne, *Responsibility and Atonement* (Oxford: Clarendon Press, 1989). Cf. especially chapter five, "Guilt, Atonement, and Forgiveness," pp. 73-92 and chapter ten, "Redemption," pp. 148-162. Also, J. Patout Burns, "The Concept of Satisfaction in Medieval Redemption Theory," *Theological Studies* 36 (1975): 285-304 for an overview of various medieval accounts of satisfaction. This article demonstrates the diversity of views in the twelfth and thirteenth centuries, illustrating both the ancient lineage of this atonement idea as well as its possible variants.

36. *The Nature of the Atonement*, p. 147.

37. *The Nature of the Atonement*, p. 135.

38. It has also been noted that there is a small tradition of Campbell interpretation which reads Campbell's theology with much greater accuracy and understanding.

39. *The Nature of the Atonement*, pp. 129,130.

40. *Institutes*, 2.16.5. It is interesting to note, however, that even in this text on Christ bearing the punishment for human sin, Calvin makes clear that the *reason* such a teaching is important is for the reassurance and confidence of believers. Calvin does not miss opportunities to emphasize the repose and certainty believers have because of the substitution of Christ. Campbell, of course, would not agree that believers can find repose in the substitutionary punishment of Christ. But he does share Calvin's concern to locate and highlight the source of that confidence and repose.

41. *Institutes*, 4.3.19.

42. *Institutes*, 4.3.20.

43. *Christ the Bread of Life*, p. 130, 135. A full treatment of Campbell's fascinating views on Christian prayer and worship is not possible here. Briefly, Campbell not only holds that Christ intercedes for us to the Father, but that the believing community worships the Father "within the circle of the life of Christ" (p. 130). Through the Spirit, the believer is so connected to Christ as to worship God in and with Christ. Cf. also T.F. Torrance, "The Mind of Christ in Worship; The Problem of Apollinarianism in the Liturgy," *Theology in Reconciliation* (London: Geoffrey Chapman, 1975), pp. 139-141.

44. *The Nature of the Atonement*, p. 368, emphasis Campbell's.

45. *The Nature of the Atonement*, p. 370.

46. Charles Partee, "Calvin's Central Dogma Again," *Calvin Studies III*, Papers of the 1986 Davidson Colloquium, ed. John Leith (Richmond: Union Theological Seminary, 1986), p. 41, "Calvin did not find a key and build a house to fit it. Calvin did not set out to expound theology from the point of view of any one doctrine. Nevertheless, the exposition of his theology finds the presence of the union with Christ in so many places and in such a significant way that "union with Christ" may be usefully taken as the central affirmation." Lewis Smedes, in *Union with Christ* (Grand Rapids: Eerdmans Publishing Company, 1983), p. 10, comes to a similar conclusion, saying that for Calvin, "a real union with Christ is indispensable for Christian existence." Smedes study is helpful not only with respect to interpreting Calvin's doctrine of the union with Christ, but also with respect to Pauline biblical materials that are the source of this doctrine for Calvin and other important voices in the tradition. Trevor Hart, in "Humankind in Christ and Christ in Humankind: Salvation as Participation in our Substitute in the Theology of John Calvin," *Scottish Journal of Theology* 42 (1989), p. 81, identifies union with Christ as "the central theme of Calvin's theology."

47. W. Kolfhaus, *Christusgemeinshaft bei Johannes Calvin* (Neukirchen: Buchhandung des Erziehungvereins, 1939), p. 12. "Ich meine nicht, dass die Lehre von der Christusgemeinschaft die Zentrallehre Calvins darstellt; wohl aber, dass sie uns wichtigen Aufschluss gibt über weite, und zwar die bedeutsamstem Gebiete des calvinischen Denkens."

48. Emil Brunner, *Von Werk des Heiligen Geistes*, 1935, p. 38, "die Mitte des Ganzen calvinischen Denkens"; David Willis-Watkins, "The Unio Mystica and the Assurance of Faith According to Calvin," *Calvin, Erbe und Auftrag: Festschrift für Wilhelm Neuser za seinem 65. Geburtstag*, ed. Willen van't Spijker (Kampen: Kok Uitgeverij, 1991), p. 2; P.J. Richel, *Het Kerkbegrip van Calvijn*, 1942), p. 56, "Voor Calvijn is deze gedachte der unio mystica van fundamenteele beteekenis voor heel zijn theologisch denken."

49. Wilhelm Niesel, *The Theology of Calvin*, trans. Harold Knight (Philadelphia: Westminster Press, 1956), p. 9.

50. Erwin Mülhaupt, *Die Predigt Calvins, ihre Geschichte, ihre Form und ihre religiösen Grundgedanken* (Berlin: de Gruyter, 1931).

51. Alexander Schweizer, *Die Glaubenslehre der evangelishce-reformierten Kirche*, 1844, F.C. Baur, *Lehrbuch der christlichen Dogmengeschichte*, 1847, and Otto Ritschl, *Dogmengeschichte des Protestantismus*, vol. 3 (Göttingen, 1926). Wendel notes that the claim of Schweizer and Baur so influenced subsequent Calvin interpretation that "historians and dogmaticians went on for three-quarters of a century repeating that affirmation like an article of faith which did not even need to be verified." Cf. Wendel, *Calvin; Origins and Development of His Religious Thought*, p. 263.

52. Alfred Göhler, *Calvins Lehre von der Heiligung* (Munich: 1934).

53. Hermann Weber, *Die Theologie Calvins; Ihre innere Systematik im Lichte structurpsychogischer Forschungsmethode* (Berlin: E. Jaensch, 1930).

54. This is Niesel's own thesis. Cf. *The Theology of Calvin*, p. 246-250. "There is hardly an aspect of theology which someone or other has not considered as quite specially typical for Calvin's doctrine. The variety of these proposals need no longer astonish us; for we have seen that Calvin was concerned to expound in all its fullness and depth the self-revelation of God to which Holy Scripture bears witness" (p. 247).

55. From W. Krusche, *Das Wirken des Heiligen Geistes nach Calvin* (Göttingen: Vandenhoeck & Ruprecht, 1957), p. 266.

56. *Institutes* 3.11.10. "Therefore, that joining together of Head and members, that indwelling of Christ in our hearts - in short, that mystical union - are accorded by us the highest degree of importance, so that Christ, having been made ours, makes us sharers with him in the gifts with which he has been endowed."

57. *Institutes* 3.1.1.

58. *Institutes*, 3.1.1.

59. Kolfhaus says, "Union with Christ means that he dwells in us and we in him, bound with one another through an unbreakable tie." (Unio cum Christo bedeutet, dass er in uns wohnt und wir in ihm sind, verbunden untereinander durch ein unzerreilssbares Band.) *Christusgemeinschaft bei Johannes Calvin*, p. 32.

60. John Calvin's Ninth Sermon of the Passion, *Corpus Reformatorum* 46, 953, quoted in Wendel, p. 235.

61. *Institutes*, 3.2.24.

62. Cf. Calvin's *De aeterna Dei praedestinatione, Corpus Reformatorum* 8, 271; quoted by Wendel, *Calvin; Origins and Development of His Religious Thought*, p. 238, " 'Those whom God now calls by the Gospel into the hope of salvation, those whom he inserts into the body of Christ', are the very same 'that he makes heirs of the life eternal, and that he has adopted in his eternal and secret counsel'."

63. Robert S. Paul, "The Atonement: Sacrifice and Penalty," p. 151.

64. *Institutes*, 2.15.6, emphasis mine.

65. *The Nature of the Atonement*, p. 152, emphasis mine.

66. *The Nature of the Atonement*, p. 126, emphasis mine. Campbell also says, "We are contented and thankful to begin our new life with partaking in the mind of Christ. . ." (p. 178).

67. *The Nature of the Atonement*, p. 155.

68. *The Nature of the Atonement*, p. 160, emphasis mine.

69. *The Nature of the Atonement*, p. 160, 161, emphasis mine.

70. T.F. Torrance, "The Mind of Christ in Worship; The Problem of Apollinarianism in the Liturgy," pp. 139-214. Torrance's primary concern in this essay is to highlight the essential place of the human mind of Christ, or, simply, the full humanity of Christ, in Christ's mediation of Christian worship. For this, he finds support in Campbell's rich theory of the connection and relationship between Christ and believers.

71. T.F. Torrance, "The Mind of Christ in Worship; The Problem of Apollinarianism in the Liturgy," p. 139.

72. John McLeod Campbell, *Christ the Bread of Life*, 2nd ed. (London: Macmillian, 1869), p. 51. Campbell develops this particular aspect of union with Christ most fully in this small book on the sacrament of the Lord's Supper. Although there are glimmers of this theme in *The Nature of the Atonement* and in his letters as collected in the *Memorials*, it is here, in *Christ the Bread of Life*, which gives Campbell interpreters the most material.

73. *Memorials*, vol. 2, p. 83.

166

74. T.F. Torrance, "The Mind of Christ in Worship; The Problem of Apollinarianism in the Liturgy," p. 141,142.

75. Cf. Paul, "The Atonement: Sacrifice and Penalty," p. 151; *Institutes*, 2.15.6.

76. *The Nature of the Atonement*, p. 182.

77. *The Nature of the Atonement*, p. 177. Campbell also links a sharing in the perfect confession of Christ with faith. In other words, when the believer shares or reproduces Christ's perfect confession, faith is made complete. "The Amen of the individual human spirit to the Amen of the Son to the mind of the Father in relation to man, is saving faith. . ." (p. 226).

78. *The Nature of the Atonement*, "The great and root-distinction of the view of the atonement presented in these pages is the relation in which our redemption is regarding as standing to the fatherliness of God. In that fatherliness has the atonement been now represented as originating. By that fatherliness has its end been represented to have been determined" (p. 338).

79. *The Nature of the Atonement*, p. 340.

80. *The Nature of the Atonement*, p. 240.

81. *The Nature of the Atonement*, p. 346.

82. *The Nature of the Atonement*, p. 347.

POSTSCRIPT

In the village of Row, on the shores of Loch Long, there is a church with a large stained glass window in memorial to John McLeod Campbell. The presence of this memorial window is not without irony; the very church which initiated Campbell's deposition now seeks to honor his memory. The window is a metaphor for the task of critical and interpretive work on Campbell. Just as the parish in Row has moved from dismissal to warm regard and pride, the small but growing body of literature on the atonement theology of John McLeod Campbell has begun to reassess the content and contribution of Campbell both to the tradition of atonement theology and the tradition of Reformed theology.

This postscript will suggest two areas for further reflection that may advance the task of Campbell interpretation and scholarship. First, it will identify and assess several limits in Campbell's atonement account and will offer suggestions for overcoming those limits or weaknesses. Second, it will suggest features or distinguishing characteristics of Campbell's atonement theology which recommend it as a lively resource for today's theological discussion.

A number of weaknesses in the presentation and argument of *The Nature of the Atonement* have already been noted.[1] This section will focus on several additional issues or questions in Campbell's atonement theology. The first, already briefly noted, is Campbell's puzzling lack of attention to Calvin. Gerrish notes ". . . one of the most curious features of Campbell's book: though it contains some harsh (and penetrating) criticisms of Calvinism, it makes no attempt whatever to deal with Calvin."[2] It is regrettable that Campbell did not link his atonement reflections with those of Calvin to strengthen his opposition to trends he had identified in both "classic Calvinism" and the "modifed Calvinists."

In addition, Campbell's zeal to replace the language of forensic externality with the language of direct religious experience of a filial relationship with God reveals a potential weakness in Campbell's account. That potential weakness can be identified as Campbell's assumption of the utter intelligibility of the atonement. That is to say, the life of Jesus Christ is, for Campbell, completely natural and comprehensible as a revelation of the reconciling will of God. The truth of the atonement, according to Campbell, is immediately and directly accessible to the inner religious intuition.[3]

Thus, some valuable features of atonement theology are muted, or even missing, in Campbell's account. Such features include a recognition of the dark mystery of the atonement, the scandal of the Incarnation, the atonement's rejection of human confidence and self-sufficiency. For Campbell, everything about the atonement seems natural, understandable, transparent. This is not to say that he rejects mystery; rather, he recognizes it. But the mystery is never the center of the atonement; it lurks at the edges of an otherwise clear and intelligible picture.

Another issue in Campbell's atonement theology concerns his use of Scripture, especially with respect to the gospel accounts of Christ's life. It is clear that Campbell has very little historical critical interest in interpreting the gospel accounts. This is evidenced by the fact that Campbell approaches the gospel accounts with a major presupposition well in place, namely, the assumption of Christ's continuous relationship of intimacy and confidence in the Father. This, for Campbell, preceeds any exegetical observation; Christ's unbroken relationship of trust and full awareness of the Father's love is an integral part of the retrospective aspect of the atonement. In that Christ is in perfect harmony with the Father, Christ witnesses to humanity of the Father's love. In that Christ experienced continual communion with the Father, Christ was able, in his perfect confession of humanity's sin, to fully feel with the Father's heart the divine judgement against sin.

Thus, much of Campbell's atonement theology depends on a certain reading of the gospel accounts of Christ's earthly experience, a reading that consistently assumes an earthly existence of perfect and unbroken awareness of God's fatherly care and faithfulness. Campbell's reading of the cry of dereliction as an expression of complete confidence and unbroken intimacy with the Father is one example of the influence of his interpretive assumptions.

It can fairly be stated that Campbell begs the question with respect to the gospel accounts of Christ's earthly life; he assumes that the narrative details of the gospel accounts will reinforce and support his presupposition that Christ's earthly life is the outward form of an inward fellowship with God. This exegetical assumption in no way invalidates the substance and content of Campbell's atonement theology, but it ought to be noted that such an exegetical assumption is no longer possible. Historical criticism has demanded of the biblical scholar and of the theologian more hermeneutical self-awareness than Campbell displayed in *The Nature of the Atonement*.

The most important issue which remains in Campbell's atonement theology is the absence of much reflection on the Holy Spirit. Although Campbell occasionally includes the Holy Spirit in his argument, sometimes even significantly, it is clear that the Spirit's role in the work of redemption is largely unexamined.

The shadowy role of the Holy Spirit in Campbell's theology affects at least three important doctrines. First, the doctrine of the Trinity is affected. Campbell lavishes so much attention on the relationship between the Father and the Son that the Spirit's participation within the divine life is rendered superfluous. A fuller development of the person of the Holy Spirit would have strengthened Campbell's Trinity doctrine. Second, the doctrine of redemption is affected. According to Campbell, one prospective benefit of Christ's sacrifice is a "partaking in the mind of Christ" and an inclusion as adopted children into the parental love of God. All the redemptive action, so to speak, occurs between the Father and the Son; the Spirit, in Campbell's theology, is given at best a supporting role. A fuller development of the person of the Holy Spirit would have strengthened Campbell's theory of the atonement as necessarily including the Spirit. The Spirit, too, has a distinctive and crucial role in the broad divine goal of redemption. Campbell, in his theory, largely fails to draw out the contours of the Spirit's part in redemption.

Third, the doctrine of the Christian life is affected. Although, as we have seen, Campbell stands in impressive continuity with Calvin on the concept of union with Christ, he lacks Calvin's thorough treatment of the Spirit's role in union with Christ. As a result, just how the Christian participates in the mind of Christ remains vague. A fuller development of the work of the Holy Spirit would have strengthened Campbell's vision of the life of the redeemed community.

The underdeveloped doctrine of the Holy Spirit in Campbell's atonement theology does not render his entire theory inadequate. In fact, a fully developed Spirit doctrine is latent, or potential, in Campbell's work. For example, on Campbell's terms, it can be said that the Spirit is the divine actor that sustained Christ's trust and intimacy with the Father, that the Spirit links the believer to the mind of Christ, that the Spirit brings the believer to share in the confession of Christ and thus share in the sacrifice of Christ, that the Spirit is the natural bridge between the retrospetive and the prospective, that the Spirit enlivens the believer's confidence of adoption into God's parental love, and that the Spirit actualized Christ's witness of the Father to humanity. These descriptions of the Holy Spirit's work are all implicit, or at least latent, in Campbell's atonement theology.

Campbell's theology is a Trinitarian theology. Although the role of the Holy Spirit is not fully developed in Campbell's account of the atonement, there is a vital sense in *The Nature of the Atonement* both of Trinitarian intimacy and cooperation in divine acts *ad intra* as well as purposeful, salvific divine activity *ad extra*. This characteristic of Campbell's theology makes him a ready participant in current theological discussion which has recently evidenced a strong interest in Trinity doctrine.

Campbell's theology is also a biblical theology. *The Nature of the Atonement* is not systematically exegetical, but the witness of the Scripture permeates and informs every aspect of Campbell's atonement discussion. As has been noted, his particular approach to Scripture has been cited as problematic for a theological generation highly sensitive to historical critical issues. But one of Campbell's foundational presuppositions, namely, his conviction that interpretation of the atonement can only rightly occur within the context of faith, is illustrated by his frequent reference to the Bible. The voice of the Bible is assumed by Campbell to be the voice of faith, the testimony of witnesses to God's faithful love and saving action. Thus, for Campbell, Scripture is a fully reliable and legitimate source for explicating the doctrine of the atonement.

Campbell's atonement theology is a church theology. The strongly prospective impulse of Campbell's theory lifts it from the confines of a pedantic theological exercise to the scope of a genuine ecclesial vision, one which provides the contours for faithful Christian witness as well as authentic Christian fellowship, both of which are founded on the believer's union with Christ.

Campbell's atonement theology is, above all, a pastoral theology, or, as one of Campbell's interpreters said, a "preachable theology."[4] Campbell was convinced that the news of Christ's redemption is good news and thus the call of the pastor is to proclaim repeatedly the love and faithfulness of God and the gift of salvation through Christ. Although *The Nature of the Atonement* was written twenty-five years after his deposition, the motivation of Campbell's life's work came from those early years. In Row, he had discovered a people anxious and fearful of their status before a judging God. Campbell's life-long pastoral efforts all focused on proclaiming the sure confidence and repose of the Christian in the light of God's redemptive activity.

In connection with this characteristic, a final related feature emerges. In that Campbell's atonement theology is pastorally oriented to troubled and restless persons, it is also a uniquely modern, or thoroughly contemporary, theology. The religious and pyschological markets of America are full of the latest remedies for the doubts, fears and struggles of searching people. But Campbell's atonement theology contains elements that meet the widespread hunger for acceptance and truth. Those elements include a consistent reassurance of God's love and mercy, a realistic appraisal of human lostness, a sturdy proclamation of the real salvific effects of Christ's life on earth, and a message of hope for present community and future wholeness. It is a message that can powerfully comfort those who search for authentic acceptance and genuine promise.

NOTES

1. Cf. chapter four. These weaknesses include the lack of attention to the biblical and patristic sources of atonement theory, a certain clumsiness in organization, argument, and style, and the peculair grouping of Owen, Edwards, and Chalmers as representative of "modified Calvinism."

2. Gerrish, *Tradition and the Modern World*, p. 91.

3. Campbell develops this idea in his first, fifth, and fourteenth chapters. He makes the claim, in the title of his fifth chapter, that the atonement is to be "seen by its own light."

4. Edgar P. Dickie, introduction to *The Nature of the Atonement*, p. xix.

BIBLIOGRAPHY

Alexander, Archibald. *The Shaping Forces of Modern Religious Thought: A History of Theological Development*. Glasgow: MacLehose, Jackson and Co., 1920.

Armstrong, Brian G. *Calvinism and the Amyraut Heresy*. Madison: The University of Wisconsin Press, 1969.

Aulen, Gustaf. *Christus Victor: An Historical Study of the Three Main Types of the Idea of the Atonement*. New York: Macmillan Publishing Co., 1969.

Baur, F.C. *Lehrbuch der christlichen Dogmengeschichte*. Leipzig: Fues, 1847.

Bell, M. Charles. *Calvin and Scottish Theology: The Doctrine of Assurance*. Edinburgh: Handsell Press, 1985.

_____. "Was Calvin a Calvinist?" *Scottish Journal of Theology* 36 (1983): 535-540.

_____. "Calvin and the Extent of the Atonement." *The Evangelical Quarterly* 55 (1983): 115-123.

Bewkes, Eugene Garrett. *Legacy of a Christian Mind*. Philadelphia: Judson Press, 1937.

Boff, Leonardo. *Passion of Christ, Passion of the World: The Facts, Their Interpretation, and Their Meaning Yesterday and Today*. Translated by Robert R. Barr. Maryknoll, New York: Orbis Books, 1987.

Brock, Rita Nakashima. *Journeys by Heart: A Christology of Erotic Power*. New York: Crossroads Publishing Company, 1988.

Brook, V.J.K. "The Atonement in Reformation Theology." *The Atonement in History and in Life*. Edited L.W. Grensted. London: SPCK, 1929.

Bruce, Alexander B. *The Humiliation of Christ*. Edinburgh: T & T Clark, 1895.

Brunner, Emil. *The Mediator: A Study of the Central Doctrine of the Christian Faith*. Trans. Olive Wyon. Philadelphia: Westminster Press, 1947.

_____. *The Christian Doctrine of Creation and Redemption*. Vol. 2. Trans. Olive Wyon. Philadelphia: Westminster Press, 1952.

_____. *Vom Werk des Heiligen Geistes*. Tübingen: Mohr, 1935.

Bushnell, Horace. *The Vicarious Sacrifice: Grounded in Principles Interpreted by Human Analogies*. New York: C. Scribner's, 1903.

_____. *Forgiveness and Law*. New York: Armstrong, 1874.

Burns, J. Patout. "The Concept of Satisfaction in Medieval Redemption Theory." *Theological Studies* 36 (1975): 284-304.

Caird, John. *The Fundamental Ideas of Christianity*. Glasgow: Maclehose, 1899.

Calvin, John. *Institutes of the Christian Religion*. Vol. 21 of *Library of Christian Classics*. Edited John T. McNeill. Translated Ford Lewis Battles. Philadelphia: Westminster Press, 1960.

Campbell, Andrew J. *Two Centuries of the Church of Scotland, 1707-1929*. Paisley: Alexander Gardner, Ltd., 1930.

Campbell, Donald. *Memorials of John McLeod Campbell, D.D.: Being Selections from his Correspondence*. London: Macmillan & Co., 1877.

Campbell, John McLeod. *The Nature of the Atonement and Its Relation to Remission of Sins and Eternal Life*, 6th ed. London: James Clarke & Co., Ltd., 1959.

_____. *Reminiscences and Reflections*. Edited by Donald Campbell. London: Macmillan and Co., 1873.

_____. *Christ the Bread of Life*. London: Macmillan and Co., 2nd ed. 1869.

_____. *Thoughts on Revelation with Special Reference to the Present Time*. 2nd ed. London: Macmillan and Co., 1874.

Carey, George. *The Gate of Glory*. London: Hodder & Stoughton, 1986.

Chambers, D. "Doctrinal Attitudes in the Church of Scotland in the Pre-Disruption Era: The Age of John McLeod Campbell and Edward Irving." *Journal of Religious History* 8 (1974): 159-182.

Dalferth, I.U. "Christ Died for Us: Reflections on the Sacrificial Language of Salvation." *Sacrifice and Redemption; Durham Essays in Theology*. Edited S.W. Sykes. Cambridge: Cambridge University Press, 1991.

Denney, James. *The Christian Doctrine of Reconciliation*. New York: George H. Doran Co., 1918.

Dictionary of National Biography, ed. Leslie Stephen and Sidney Lee. Vol. xvii, p. 494. Oxford: Oxford University Press, 1973.

Dillistone, F.W. *The Christian Understanding of Atonement*. Philadelphia: Westminster Press, 1968.

_____. *Jesus Christ and His Cross: Studies on the Saving Work of Christ*. Philadelphia: Westminster Press, 1953.

Dowey, Edward A. *The Knowledge of God in Calvin's Theology*. New York: Columbia University Press, 1952.

Dragas, George Dion. "St. Athanasius on Christ's Satisfaction." *Sacrifice and Redemption: Durham Essays in Theology*. Edited Stephen W. Sykes. Cambridge: Cambridge University Press, 1991.

Drummond, Andrew and Bulloch, James. *The Church in Victorian Scotland, 1843-1874*. Edinburgh: The Saint Andrew Press, 1975.

Dumas, André. "La Mort du Christ: N'Est-elle pas Sacrificielle?" *Etudes theologiques et religieuses* 56 (1981): 577-591.

Enright, William G. "Urbanization and the Evangelical Pulpit in Nineteenth-Century Scotland." *Church History* 47 (1978): 400-407.

Erskine, Thomas. *The Brazen Serpect*. Edinburgh: Waugh and Innes, 1831.

_____. *Remarks on the Internal Evidence for the Truth of Revealed Religion*, 4th ed. Edinburgh: Waugh and Innes, 1821.

_____. *Essay on Faith*, 4th ed. Edinburgh: Waugh and Innes, 1825.

_____. *The Unconditional Freeness of the Gospel*, 3rd ed. Edinburgh: Waugh and Innes, 1829.

Essays and Reviews. London: J.W. Parker, 1860.

Feenstra, Ronald J. and Plantinga, Jr., Cornelius, eds. *Trinity, Incarnation, and Atonement: Philosophical and Theological Essays*. Notre Dame: University of Notre Dame Press, 1989.

Fiddes, Paul. *Past Event and Present Salvation: The Christian Idea of Atonement*. Louisville: Westminster/John Knox Press, 1989.

Forsyth, P.T. *The Work of Christ*. London: Hodder & Stoughton, 1909.

Franks, Robert S. *The Atonement*. Oxford: Oxford University Press, 1934.

Franks, Robert S. *The Work of Christ: A Historical Study of Christian Doctrine*. London: Thomas Nelson and Sons, Ltd., 1962.

Galbraith, Iain B. *A Village Heritage*. Rhu and Shandon Kirk Session publication, 1981.

Gerrish, Brian. *Tradition and the Modern World: Reformed Theology in the Nineteenth Century*. Chicago: The University of Chicago Press, 1978.

_____. "The Lord's Supper in the Reformed Confessions." *Theology Today* 23 (July, 1966): 224-243.

Göhler, Alfred. *Calvins Lehre von der Heiligung*. Munich: C. Kaiser, 1934.

Goodloe, James. *John McLeod Campbell, the Atonement, and the Transformation of the Religious Consciousness*. University of Chicago Ph.D. dissertation, 1987.

Grensted, L.W. *A Short History of the Doctrine of the Atonement*. Manchester: Longmans, Green & Co., 1920.

Gunton, Colin. *The Actuality of Atonement: A Study of Metaphor, Rationality, and the Christian Tradition.* Grand Rapids: Eerdmans Publishing Company, 1989.

Hanna, William, ed. *Letters of Thomas Erskine of Linlathen.* 2 vol. New York: G.P. Putnam's Sons, 1877.

Hart, Trevor A. "Anselm of Canterbury and John McLeod Campbell: Where Opposites Meet?" *The Evangelical Quarterly* 62 (1990): 311-333.

Hart, Trevor A. "Humankind in Christ and Christ in Humankind: Salvation as Participation in Our Substitute in the Theology of John Calvin." *Scottish Journal of Theology* 42 (1989): 67-84.

Hazlett, W. Ian P. "The Scots Confession 1560: Context, Complexion and Critique." *Archiv für Reformationsgeschichte* 78 (1987): 287-320.

Helm, Paul. "Calvin, English Calvinism and the Logic of Doctrinal Development." *Scottish Journal of Theology* 34 (1981): 179-185.

_____. "Calvin and the Covenant: Unity and Continuity." *The Evangelical Quarterly* 55 (1983): 65-81.

Henderson, Henry F. *The Religious Controversies of Scotland.* Edinburgh: T & T Clark, 1905.

Hendry, George. *The Gospel of the Incarnation.* Philadelphia: Westminster Press, 1958.

Hodgson, Leonard. *The Doctrine of the Atonement.* New York: Charles Scribner's Sons, 1951.

Hughes, Thomas H. *The Atonement: Modern Theories of the Doctrine.* London: George Allen & Unwin, Ltd., 1949.

Hunt, John. *Religious Thought in England in the Nineteenth Century.* London: Gibbings & Co., Ltd., 1896.

Hort, Arthur F. *The Life and Letters of F.J.A. Hort.* London: Macmillan and Co., Ltd., 1896.

Irving, Edward. *The Collected Writings of Edward Irving.* Edited by G. Carlyle. Vol. 5: *The Doctrine of the Incarnation.* London: Alexander Strahan, 1866.

Jenkyn, Thomas W. *The Extent of the Atonement in its Relation to God and the Universe.* Boston: Gould, Kendall and Lincoln, 1846.

Jinkins, Michael. *A Comparative Study in the Theology of Atonement in Jonathan Edwards and John McLeod Campbell.* San Francisco: Mellen Research University Press, 1993.

Kelly, J.N.D. *Early Christian Doctrine.* New York: Harper & Row, 1978.

Kendall, R.T. *Calvin and English Calvinism to 1649.* Oxford: University of Oxford Press, 1979.

Kettler, Christian D. *The Vicarious Humanity of Christ and the Reality of Salvation.* Lanham, Maryland: University Press of America, Inc., 1991.

————. "The Vicarious Repentance of Christ in the Theology of John McLeod Campbll and R.C. Moberly." *Scottish Journal of Theology* 38 (1985): 529-543.

Kolfhaus, *Christusgemeinschaft bei Johannes Calvin.* Neukirchen: Buchhandung des Erziehungvereins, 1939.

Krusche, *Das Wirken des Heiligen Geistes nach Calvin.* Göttingen: Vandenhoeck & Ruprecht, 1957.

Lachman, David C. *The Marrow Controversy, 1718-1723.* Edinburgh: Rutherford House Books, 1988.

Lampe, G.W.H. and MacKinnon, D.M. *The Resurrection: A Dialogue.* Philadelphia: Westminster Press, 1966.

Lane, Tony. "The Quest for the Historical Calvin." *Evangelical Quarterly* 55 (1983): 95-113.

Lascaris, A.F. "De verzoeningsleer en het offerchristendom." *Nederlands Theologische Tijdschrift* 42 (1988): 220-242.

Leckie, J.H. "John McLeod Campbell's 'The Nature of the Atonement'." *The Expository Times* 40 (1928-1929): 198-204.

Letham, R.W.A. *Saving Faith and Assurance in Reformed Theology: Zwingli to the Synod of Dort.* 1979 Aberdeen University Ph.D. thesis.

Lewis, C.S. *Mere Christianity.* New York: Macmillan, 1958.

Lias, J.J. *The Atonement Viewed in the Light of Certain Modern Difficulties.* 2nd Ed. London: James Nisbet & Co., 1888.

Macaulay, A.B. *The Death of Jesus.* London: Hodder & Stoughton, 1938.

MacGregor, Geddes. "The Row Heresy." *Harvard Theological Review* 43 (1985): 281-301.

Macleod, John. *Scottish Theology in Relation to Church History Since the Reformation.* Edinburgh: The Banner of Truth Trust, 1974.

MacKinnon, Donald. "The Conflict Between Realism and Idealism." *Explorations in Theology 5.* London: SCM Press, Ltd., 1979.

_____. "Subjective and Objective Conceptions of Atonement." *Prospect for Theology.* Edited F.G. Healey. Digswell Place, Hertfordshire: James Nisbet & Co., Ltd., 1966.

Mackintosh, H.R. *Some Aspects of Christian Belief.* London: Hodder and Stoughton, 1924.

Macquarrie, John. "John McLeod Campbell, 1800-1872." *The Expository Times* 83 (1972): 263-268.

_____. *Jesus Christ in Modern Thought.* London: SCM Press, 1990.

_____. *Thinking About God.* London: SCM Press, Ltd., 1975.

Mansel, Henry L. *The Limits of Religious Thought Examined.* Oxford: J. Wright, 1858.

Martineau, James. "Mediatorial Religion." *Studies of Christianity: Timely Thoughts for Religious Thinkers.* Edited W.R. Alger. Boston: American Unitarian Association, 1875.

Mather, G.B. "The Atonement: Representative or Substitutionary?" *Canadian Journal of Theology* 4 (1958): 266-272.

Maurice, F.D. *What is Revelation?* London: Macmillan and Co., 1859.

McCoy, Charles S. and Baker, J. Wayne. *Fountainhead of Federalism: Heinrich Bullinger and the Covenantal Tradition.* Louisville: Westminster/John Knox Press, 1991.

McGrath, Alister, "The Moral Theory of the Atonement: An Historical and Theological Critique." *Scottish Journal of Theology* 38 (1985): 205-220.

_____. "John Calvin and Late Mediaeval Thought." *Archiv für Reformationgeschichte* 77 (1986): 58-78.

_____. "Homo Assumptus?: A Study in the Christology of the via moderna, with particular reference to William of Ockham." *Ephemerides Theologicae Lovaniensis* 60 (1984): 283-297.

_____. *The Intellectual Origins of the European Reformation.* Oxford: Blackwell Publishers, 1987.

Mechie, Stewart. "The Marrow Controversy Reviewed." *The Evangelical Quarterly* 22 (1950): 20-31.

Moberly, Robert C. *Atonement and Personality.* London: Duckworth & Co., 1915.

Morris, Thomas V. *The Logic of God Incarnate.* Ithaca, NY: Cornell University Press, 1986.

Morrison, N. Brysson. *They Need No Candle: Builders of Presbyterianism in Scotland 1500-1950.* Richmond: John Knox Press, 1957.

Mozley, J.K. *The Doctrine of the Atonement.* New York: Charles Scribner's Sons, 1916.

_____. *Some Tendencies in British Theology.* London: SPCK, 1951.

Mülhaupt, Erwin. *Die Predigt Calvins, ihre Geschichte, ihre Form und ihre religiösen Grundgedanken.* Berlin: de Gruyter, 1931.

New Dictionary of Theology. Edited Sinclair B. Ferguson and David Wright. Downers Grove, IL: InterVarsity Press, 1988. "John McLeod Campbell," I. Hamilton, pp. 126,127.

Niesel, *The Theology of Calvin.* Trans. Harold Knight. Philadelphia: Westminster Press, 1956.

Partee, Charles. "Calvin's Central Dogma Again." *Calvin Studies III,* Papers of the 1986 Davidson Colloquium. Ed. John Leith. Richmond: Union Theological Seminary, 1986.

Paul, Robert S. *The Atonement and the Sacraments* New York: Abingdon Press, 1960.

_____. "The Atonement: Sacrifice and Penalty." *Readings in Calvin's Theology.* Edited Donald K. McKim. Grand Rapids: Baker Book House, 1985.

Pauw, Amy Plantinga. *"The Supreme Harmony of All": Jonathan Edwards and the Trinity.* 1990 Yale University Ph.D. dissertation.

Pfleiderer, Otto. *The Development of Theology in Germany Since Kant and its Progress in Great Britain Since 1825,* 3rd ed. Trans. J. Frederick Smith. London: Swan Sonnenschein & Co., 1909.

Rashdall, Hastings. *The Idea of Atonement in Christian Theology.* London: Macmillan & Co., 1920.

Reardon, Bernard M.G. *From Coleridge to Gore: A Century of Religious Thought in Britain.* London: Longman Group, Ltd., 1971.

Richel, P.J. *Het Kerkbegrip van Calvijn.* Utrecht: Libertas Drukkerigen, 1942.

Ritschl, Otto. *Dogmengeschichte des Protestantismus.* Vol. 4. Göttingen: Vandenhoeck & Ruprecht, 1927.

Robertson, William. *The Works of William Robertson.* 2 vol. Vol. 1: "The Situation of the World at the Time of Christ's Appearance, and Its Connexions with the Success of His Religion Considered." London: W. Ball, 1840.

Rolston, Holmes. *John Calvin versus the Westminster Confession.* Richmond: John Knox Press, 1972.

Rupp, George. *Christologies and Cultures: Toward a Typology of Religious Worldviews.* The Hague: Mouton & Co., 1974.

Sanday, William. *Christologies Ancient and Modern.* New York: Oxford University Press, American Branch, 1910.

Schweizer, A. *Die Glaubenslehre der Evangelish-reformierten Kirche.* Zurich: Orell, Füssli und Comp, 1844.

Sher, Richard and Murdoch, Alexander. "Patronage and Party in the Church of Scotland, 1750-1800." *Church, Politics and Society.* Edited Norman Macdougall. Edinburgh: John Donald Publishers, Ltd., 1983.

Sher, Richard. *Church and University in the Scottish Enlightenment: The Moderate Literati of Edinburgh.* Princeton: Princeton University Press, 1985.

Smedes, Lewis. *Union with Christ.* Grand Rapids: Eerdmans Publishing Company, 1983.

Smith, John Pye. *Four Discourses on the Sacrifice and Priesthood of Jesus Christ and the Atonement and Redemption Thence Accruing,* 4th ed. Edinburgh: William Oliphant & Co., 1859.

Stevens, G.B. *Christian Doctrine of Salvation.* New York: Charles Scribner's Son, 1905.

Story, Robert H. *Memoir of the Life of the Reverend Robert Story.* London: Macmillan & Co., 1862.

Stott, John R.W. *The Cross of Christ.* Downers Grove, Ill: InterVarsity Press, 1986.

Surin, Kenneth. "Atonement and Christology." *Neue Zeitschrift für Theologie und Religionsphilosophie* 24 (1982): 131-149.

Swinburne, Richard. *Responsibility and Atonement.* Oxford: Clarendon Press, 1989.

Taylor, Vincent. *Jesus and His Sacrifice.* London: Macmillan & Co., 1955.

_____. "The Best Books on the Atonement." *The Expository Times* 48 (Oct. 1936-Sep. 1937): 267-273.

Taylor, Vincent. *The Atonement in New Testament Teaching.* London: Epworth Press, 1954.

Thimell, Daniel P. "Christ in Our Place in the Theology of John McLeod Campbell." *Christ in Our Place: The Humanity of God in Christ for the Reconciliation of the World.* Edited Trevor Hart and Daniel Thimell. Exeter: Paternoster Press, 1989.

Torrance, James B. "The Contribution of McLeod Campbell to Scottish Theology." *Scottish Journal of Theology* 26 (1973): 295-311.

_____. "The Vicarious Humanity of Christ." *The Incarnation.* Ed. T.F. Torrance. Edinburgh: Handsell Press, 1981.

_____. "The Incarnation and 'Limited Atonement'." *The Evangelical Quarterly* 55 (1983): 83-94.

Torrance, Thomas F. "The Mind of Christ in Worship: The Problem of Apollinarianism in the Liturgy." *Theology in Reconciliation.* London: Geoffrey Chapman Publishers, 1975.

_____. *The Trinitarian Faith: The Evangelical Theology of the Ancient Catholic Church.* Edinburgh: T & T Clark, 1988.

Tuttle, George. *So Rich a Soil: John McLeod Campbell on Christian Atonement.* Edinburgh: Handsel Press, 1986.

Van Buren, Paul M. *A Theology of the Jewish Christian Reality: Christ in Context.* San Francisco: Harper & Row, 1988.

_____. *Christ in Our Place: The Substitutionary Character of Calvin's Doctrine of Reconciliation.* Edinburgh: Oliver & Boyd, 1957.

Walker, James. *Theology and Theologians of Scotland 1560-1750.* Edinburgh: Knox Press, 1982.

Wardlaw, Ralph. *Discourses on the Nature and Extent of the Atonement of Christ.* Glasgow: James Maclehose, 1844.

Warfield, Benjamin Breckinridge. *The Person and Work of Christ.* Philadelphia: The Presbyterian and Reformed Publishing Company, 1950.

Webb, Clement. *A Study of Religious Thought in England from 1850.* Oxford: Clarendon Press, 1933.

Weber, Hermann. *Die Theologie Calvins; Ihre innere Systematik im Lichte structurpsychogischer Forschungsmethode.* Berlin: E. Jaensch, 1930.

Wells, David. *Search for Salvation.* Leicester: InterVarsity Press, 1978.

Wendell, Francois. *Calvin: Origins and Development of His Religious Thought.* New York: Harper & Row, 1963.

Williams, Daniel Day. *The Spirit and the Forms of Love.* New York: Harper & Row, 1968.

Willis, E. David. *Calvin's Catholic Christology; the Function of the So-Called Extra Calvinisticum in Calvin's Theology.* Leiden: E.J. Brill, 1966.

Willis-Watkins, E. David. "The Unio Mystica and the Assurance of Faith According to Calvin." *Calvin, Erbe und Auftrag: Festschrift für Wilhelm Neuser zu seinem 65. Geburtstag.* Ed. Willem van't Spijker. Kampen: Kok Uitgeverij, 1991.

The Whole Proceedings Before the Presbytery of Dumbarton and Ayr, in the Case of the Rev. John McLeod Campbell, Minister of Row. Greenock: R.B. Lusk, 1831.

INDEX